JUDGES–KINGS

The Storyteller's Companion to the Bible

Michael E. Williams, editor
VOLUME THREE

JUDGES–KINGS

Abingdon Press
Nashville

JUDGES—KINGS

This book is printed on recycled, acid-free paper.

$20.00

Library of Congress Cataloging-in-Publication Data

The Storyteller's companion to the Bible.   3/99
    Includes indexes.
    Contents: v. 1. Genesis—v. 2. Exodus-Joshua—v. 3. Judges-Kings.
        1. Bible—Pharaphrases, English. 2. Bible—Criticism, interpretation, etc.
    I. Williams, Michael E. (Michael Edward), 1950-   .
    BS550.2.S764   1991   220.9'505   90-26289
    ISBN 0-687-39670-0 (v. 1   :   alk. paper)
    ISBN 0-687-39671-9 (v. 2   :   alk. paper)
    ISBN 0-687-39672-7 (v. 3   :   alk. paper)

MANUFACTURED IN THE UNITED STATES OF AMERICA

As always
for
Margaret
and
Sarah
and
in memory of
Abraham Goldberg
(1901–1992)

Contributors

David Penchansky teaches in the Department of Theology at the University of Saint Thomas in St. Paul, Minnesota. He holds a Ph.D. in Hebrew Bible from Vanderbilt University. He is the author of *Betrayal of God* (Westminster/John Knox, 1991).

David Albert Farmer is pastor of University Baptist Church in Baltimore, Maryland, and editor of *Pulpit Digest*. He is the author of two books, *And Blessed Is She: Sermons by Women* (Harper, San Francisco, 1990) and *Basic Bible Sermons on Hope* (Broadman, 1991).

Shelley Gotterer earned her M.A. in Oral Interpretation from Northwestern University. She is a storyteller and coordinator of the fine arts program at Westminster School, a school for children with learning disabilities in Nashville, Tennessee.

Michael E. Williams earned his Ph.D. from Northwestern University. He is one of the pastors of Belle Meade United Methodist Church in Nashville, Tennessee, and former Director of Preaching for The United Methodist Church. He presently is establishing the Center for Religious Imagination as a network for educators and pastors who seek to spread the good news through story.

Contents

CONTENTS

A Storyteller's Companion

Michael E. Williams

This volume, like the previous two in the Storyteller's Companion to the Bible Series, is for anyone interested in telling Bible stories. In this volume we focus our attention on stories from Judges through 1 Kings. Pastors who have preaching responsibilities will find this book particularly helpful as they prepare to tell one of these stories as part of a sermon. If preaching is to help the listener to participate in the world of the biblical narrative, then telling stories from the Bible is imperative.

In addition, leaders of Bible studies and teachers of church school classes will invariably be called upon to tell Bible stories as part of their lessons. The first two volumes have been used for personal Bible study by many individuals looking for alternative resources for enriching their knowledge of Scripture. It may be that parents and grandparents will want to tell portions of these or other biblical stories at other times, too.

Almost all of the stories collected here are *adult* stories. In part this is because they deal with issues and actions that are not a part of a child's realm of experience. The traditions of the Hebrew Bible can be brutally honest about its characters. None of them are portrayed as being flawless, and sometimes their behavior is troubling to readers looking for moral exemplars or pious forebears.

The issue here is not simply that God can choose flawed individuals to do a divine work. It seems in many of these stories that God has a penchant for employing people who are the least likely to be heroic in the way our culture, or theirs, expects. Samson the strong has a weakness for Philistine women. Gideon, one of the least qualified persons ever chosen to lead an army, has the audacity to put God to the test. The best-known example is David, who abuses his royal power by impregnating a woman and then having the woman's husband killed.

Through these stories we enter a world much like our own. It is the kind of world where a drunken, brawling Dylan Thomas can pen the lyrical poem, "Fern Hill." Or the master of short and long fiction, John Cheever, is revealed by his children's recollections and his own journals to have been a deplorable husband, as conflicted in his sexuality as he was clear in his prose. It is a world in which candidates running for office had best be prepared for every detail of their private lives to be revealed.

A modern attempt to explore some of the same issues found in the Bible stories is Peter Schaffer's *Amadeus*. A bewildered Salieri wonders how God could gift such a precocious, spoiled brat as Mozart with such genius. Though Salieri devotes himself with a godly discipline and devotion to music, he recognizes that his gift pales next to that of Mozart. Why in the world would God gift such flawed people with such enormous gifts? We may never know, except that such choices emphasize the uncanny freedom with which the surprising YHWH works. The less complex answer to why God chooses imperfect people to do a divine work is that we are the only kind of people available.

The Stories

This volume offers an overview of the time of the judges through the establishment of the monarchy with Saul, the reigns of David, Solomon, and their successors. Obviously, we could not deal in detail with every verse of all the books between Judges and 1 Kings. We have included the passages that appear in the lectionaries, including the *Revised Common Lectionary 1992*. Beyond these texts we included those stories that seemed to make a significant contribution to the narrative as a whole.

If you do not happen to find one of your favorite stories in this collection, there is no need to despair. Much of the information you will learn from the comments on the stories that are included can be transferred to other texts. This will allow you to use your creativity even more fully.

The translation from which the printed texts in this companion are taken is *The Revised English Bible*. You may wish to compare the readings here with your favorite translation or several others. It enriches the telling of biblical stories, especially for those who do not read the original language, to work from various translations.

Comments on the Stories

David Penchansky teaches in the Department of Theology at the University of Saint Thomas in St. Paul, Minnesota. He holds a Ph.D. in Hebrew Bible from Vanderbilt University. As our scholar, he reminds us that every story is told from someone's point of view. That in itself shapes and colors how the characters are portrayed and how the events of the story are described. He also keeps before the reader the fact that stories about leaders always have a political perspective as well. We know this is true for our time. For example, it is usually clear whether someone describing the policies of a sitting president is a member of that president's political party. David does not try to reduce the ambiguity present in the stories by giving simple answers to complicated situations. He does not tell you how to tell the story, but rather provides you with the information you need to choose how you will tell the stories.

The specific contribution you will make to the preparation for telling one of these stories is knowing your audience. You can take the information David Penchansky offers and shape a telling of the story that will be appropriate to the ages and life experiences of your listeners. Only you can know where in the lives of those in your congregation, class, or family a story will strike a chord, turn on a light, or heal a hurt. For more information on how to prepare a story for a specific group of listeners, refer to "Learning to Tell Bible Stories: A Self-directed Workshop" on pages 21-22.

Retelling the Stories

As a storyteller, you will contribute something of your own personality and understanding of the Bible and your listeners to the telling of a Bible story. There is no one right way to accomplish this. While this companion includes sample retellings of each story, these are only examples of one way a story may be told. You may choose to tell it very differently.

The retellings are intended to free your imagination for telling and not to limit you to any one form. Some retellings here are fairly straightforward recountings of a text. Others choose a character or characters from whose point of view to tell the story. Some retellings place the story in the modern world. We hope they will offer you a sample of the vast number of ways Bible stories can come to life in storytelling.

The goal of each retelling is to help our listeners to hear the story as if for the first time and to see the world of the story as something new and fresh. We are grateful for the imaginations of the storytellers who provided the retellings in this volume: David Albert Farmer is pastor of University Baptist Church in Baltimore, Maryland, and editor of *Pulpit Digest*. He retold the first eight stories in this collection. Shelley Gotterer is a storyteller and coordinator of the fine arts program at Westminster School, a school for children with learning disabilities in Nashville, Tennessee. She retold the next eleven stories. Finally, I retold the last nine stories.

Midrashim

If you ask a rabbi a question, you are very likely to get a story for an answer. This reflects a wisdom that knows truth to be irreducible to a one-two-three answer. Truth is embodied in events as they happen and in persons as they relate to each other and to God. This kind of truth is best experienced in stories and concrete images. Perhaps no book is a better example of this storied truth telling than the Bible.

The most unique contribution this companion makes to the art of biblical storytelling is to include the stories and sayings of the ancient rabbis related to the Judges—1 Kings narrative. These are midrashim (the singular is midrash), from a Hebrew word that means "to go in search of." When the rabbis went in search of the relevance of these already "old, old stories" for their time, they returned with questions. Those questions generated stories that stand alongside the Scripture passages and interpret them in ways that children and adults alike can understand.

The midrashim included here came from several sources, and I have retold and adapted them for inclusion here. These midrashim appear in boxed text in the retelling of each story, placed near the part of the story to which it most closely relates. As you retell the story, you may wish to include one of the midrashim at these points in the story or at other appropriate places. For more information, refer to "What Are Midrashim, and What Are They Doing Here?" on pages 17-19.

You will probably not want to read this companion from front to back as you would most books. It was not designed to be read that way. One way to make effective use of it would be first to read David Penchansky's introduction to his comments on the stories and the introduction to midrash. Then choose a story that you wish to tell. This may be a story from an upcoming Sunday of the lectionary or the church school curriculum, or it may simply be a story that captures your interest. Once you have chosen the story, work through the short workshop on storytelling, using the story you chose as your content.

Use the retelling provided with the story as a guide, but do not feel obligated to simply repeat it. Tell the story for your hearers in your own way. You may choose to include the midrashim with your retelling, or you may tell them afterward. In any case, you are about to take part in one of the most ancient experiences people do in community: offering the gift of God's story so that it touches our story today.

Reading the Narratives of Judges—Kings

David Penchansky

> The Israelites did what was evil in the sight of [YHWH], forgetting [YHWH] their God, and worshiping the Baals and the Asherahs. Therefore the anger of [YHWH] was kindled against Israel, and he sold them into the hand of King Cushan-rishathaim.... But when the Israelites cried out to [YHWH], [YHWH] raised up a deliverer for the Israelites.... The spirit of [YHWH] came upon [Othniel], and he judged Israel; he went out to war. (Judges 3:7-10)

The comments in this volume concern a portion of what scholars call Deuteronomic history, which comprises the works of Joshua, Judges, 1 and 2 Samuel, and 1 and 2 Kings. These passages are collected and woven together because they share a common theological viewpoint expressed cogently in the above quote. The God who called the Israelites in the Exodus and promised to be their God and fight for them would abandon them for religious unfaithfulness, but would return in power if they only repented.

The Deuteronomist, writing in a time of grave Israelite defeat and discouragement, insisted that it was not God's fault that the Israelites were defeated. In ancient times, when two nations fought, it was believed that the gods of those nations fought as well; if a nation was defeated, the god of that nation suffered the reproach. But the Deuteronomist, drawing from the theological perspective of the book of Deuteronomy, insisted that Israelite defeats were not the result of the failure of Israel's God, but rather of their own failure to adequately serve their God.

Although this seems like a stinging rebuke to those who found themselves wrenched from their land and forced to serve foreign oppressors, it enabled the people to keep their faith with their deity. As long as YHWH's love was neither inconstant nor inadequate, there remained the possibility of a return: a return of Israel to their God and a return of their God in gracious restoration.

The Deuteronomist, writing perhaps in the sixth century B.C.E., had available an enormous wealth of written and oral material: early legends and folk tales, court histories, military histories, and royal chronicles. The writer wove them together with varying degrees of skill into a single work that brought forth the Deuteronomic theological perspective. Each individual story, however, had its own context, its own theological and historical purposes, often at significant variance with the Deuteronomic perspective as well as with each other.

What remains is a rich and complex tapestry, subject to various readings and interpretations, the parts relating tensively to the whole. I have attempted to bring out the diverse perspectives, occasionally highlighting those that might be lost, were one to read all through the light of this later editor.

I chose these passages because they were disturbing. Many of them do not readily provide a simple, cut-and-dried moral lesson, and what lessons they might offer are often too difficult to bear. Many religious communities have given lip service to these passages. They must, because the stories are included in the sacred canon, but in practice we usually either avoid them or domesticate them through harmonizing and misleading interpretations. To render these stories tame is a disservice to them, robbing them of their life and interest. They cease to challenge or change lives. Rather, they only confirm the readers and hearers in old prejudices and comforting religious categories.

When these stories were told the first time, they tore the hearer loose from old assumptions and perceptions—and it suddenly became possible for those listening to make entirely new connections. But the impact of such stories has a short shelf life in their pristine form—they rapidly develop accretions— explanations that tell later readers what the stories mean. An example of this process from the New Testament is Jesus' parable of the sower (Mark 4:1-20), which is provided with an interpretive key by a "helpful" editor explaining what each of the soils "means."

Almost an infinite number of radical possibilities might occur in the act of hearing or reading a story, depending on the reader's history, what she or he brings to a story, and the kinds of cues offered by the storyteller. However, when you announce what a story means you eliminate all possible interpretations other than the one you provide.

This is both the danger and the glory of these stories—danger because the response to hearing or reading these stories might be different from what we intend, and glorious because if we lose control of the text and its interpretation, features within the story itself begin to take charge of the interpretive process. We begin to hear and see aspects of the text we never were aware of before.

So I commend to you these stories, many of them difficult and ambiguous, and I urge you to tell them in ways that retain that ambiguity. Do not wrap them up in neat packages tied with ribbon, but rather leave them rough-hewn and unfinished, unresolved and difficult.

As you prepare, seek to render the story an experience felt by your listeners. If you allow them to care deeply for the characters, be moved by their elation or struck dumb by their pain, you have more than succeeded in telling the story well.

These stories carry power and can powerfully affect those who process them. Tell them in a fashion that will allow your listeners to experience that power.

Most English translations insert "LORD" whenever the Hebrew word *YHWH* appears. *YHWH,* however, is the personal name of the God of Israel, and the name must be used in order to distinguish him from the other ancient Near Eastern gods. The name was probably pronounced *YAH-way.* I will use YHWH when it is relevant for understanding the story. It is the proper name for a character in the narratives, in this case, the Israelite God. YHWH is not strictly male, but I will follow the traditional use of male pronouns when referring to him.

I have often paraphrased or used my own translations throughout my retelling of these tales. When I quote a translation, it is from the New Revised Standard Version. I have replaced their use of LORD with YHWH for consistency, and I will indicate the exact biblical reference.

What Are Midrashim, and
What Are They Doing Here?

Michael E. Williams

Midrash (the plural in Hebrew is *midrashim*) comes from a Hebrew word meaning "to go in search of" or "to inquire." So midrashim resulted when the ancient rabbis went in search of (inquired into) the meaning of the Scriptures for their lives. Midrash is also the name for the process of inquiring into the Scriptures for their meaning.

We might say that midrash is both our encounter with the biblical stories as we seek their meaning for our lives and times and the stories that emerge to express that meaning. Often midrashim do take the form of stories or pieces of stories (at least the ones we will focus on here do). These stories seek to answer questions about and to fill gaps in the biblical stories.

The midrashim drawn from for this volume come from the period 400–1200 C.E. (what is sometimes called A.D.). They were told, in part, to make the stories of Judges—Kings relevant to a Jewish community that had no homeland, could not hold citizenship in other countries, and experienced hostility and persecution from the outside, including from Christian authorities. Most of these midrashim originated in sermons preached in synagogues, based on the prescribed weekly readings from the Torah (the first five books of the Bible). Others emerged from the popular folk traditions of the Jewish communities. Though they were collected and written during that six-hundred-year period, there is no way of knowing how long the midrashim had been circulating by word of mouth before someone wrote them down. Some are attributed to rabbis living at the time of Jesus. In fact, certain scholars find evidence that this way of interpreting the Bible has its roots intertwined with the texts of the biblical stories themselves.

I see three basic functions for the midrashim I have selected to be included in this book. The first might be called "filling the gaps." These stories and story fragments answer questions about the biblical stories that the Scripture leaves unanswered. For example, why was the boy David chosen to be king over all his older brothers? What happened to Elijah, since he never died? When the rabbis answered such questions, they revealed both their fertile imaginations and their own understanding of God and human beings. Sunday school teachers and college professors will also have encountered these imaginative questions.

The second function of midrash is to draw an analogy. These stories begin with "This may be compared to. . . . " Then the rabbi would tell a contemporary story that exhibited a situation and characters like the biblical story under consideration. You may notice that these stories sometimes bear a resemblance to the parables of Jesus and the *mashal* (parable) form of Jewish teaching.

The third function is to describe an encounter. In these stories someone comes to a rabbi with a question, and the rabbi's response interprets both the biblical story and the situation from which the question emerged. For example, when someone asked a rabbi how Ruth, a Moabite woman, could have been the great-grandmother of King David, since Deuteronomy prohibits a Moabite from ever becoming a member of the community, the rabbi responded that the law said Moabite, not Moabitess.

Why did I choose a predominantly Jewish form of interpretation in this book? First, Christians have too often ignored this ancient and time-honored way to interpret the Bible. Given our Jewish roots and Jesus' heritage, midrash is at least as directly related to our tradition as the Greco-Roman philosophy on which we have depended so heavily for ordering our questions and structuring our theological doctrines.

Second, midrashim provide us with a way of interpreting the Bible that involves the imagination and speaks to our experience. It is also, according to certain scholars, the way the Bible interprets itself.

Third, midrashim provide a model for a community-based, inclusive (even children can imaginatively participate in stories), nonprofessional (you don't have to be a trained theologian) way of interpreting the Bible for our times. In short, we can learn the stories the rabbis told about the scriptures to interpret them for their time. In addition, we can follow the example of the rabbis and learn to tell stories about Bible stories that interpret them for our time.

In addition to these reasons I have a personal appreciation for the Jewish storytelling tradition. Though my intellectual and artistic interests in Jewish narrative range from the Torah to midrash to hasidic stories to modern writers such as Isaac Bashevis Singer and Elie Wiesel, my heart's response to Judaism and its stories had its birth in my relationship with one person, my uncle Abraham Goldberg.

Growing up in rural Tennessee, my young life was hardly an experience of religious diversity. Until I left home for college, Abe was the only Jewish person I had ever met. Even then I knew him only from brief encounters. He would accompany my father's sister, Aunt Mary, and my cousins, Karen and Susan, on their summer visits to Tennessee. While his wife and daughters would stay for several weeks, after a few days my only contact with the Jewish world would return to Chicago and his hardware business.

I do not recall my Uncle Abe ever telling me a story. I do, however, remember this tall, bald, gentle man and his kindness and openness to others. Through his tolerance of those whose backgrounds were different from his own, Abraham Goldberg generated in me respect, not simply for an individual, but for the God, culture, and people that could produce such a man as he.

This is just the first step to reclaiming midrashim for modern tellers of Bible stories, but it is a step. If you want to learn more about midrashim related to the stories of Judges—Kings, you may wish to read the volumes from which those included here were chosen.

Midrash Rabbah, translated by H. Freedman (London: Soncino Press, 1939), is a ten-volume translation of midrashim on a variety of books of the Bible. There references here, which have been paraphrased and adapted, are to chapter and section. The third edition of this work was published in 1983.

Louis Ginzberg's classic collection of stories related to biblical texts, *The Legends of the Jews,* translated by Henrietta Szold (Philadelphia: The Jewish Publication Society, 1909 and 1937), still in print, draws from a wide number of sources, including Christian and Islamic traditions. Here this work, again paraphrased and adapted, is listed as Ginzberg, followed by the volume and page number.

Another source I have employed is *The Antiquities of the Jews,* by Flavius Josephus. Here again I have paraphrased and adapted these passages and refer to them by book, chapter, and section.

One more word on midrash: For any given passage of Scripture, several stories or interpretations of various rabbis are presented side by side in collections of midrashim. Those who collected these stories saw no reason to decide which was the one right interpretation. This is also true, we might mention, of those who assembled the canon of the New Testament, who saw no reason to choose among the four very different stories about Rabbi Jesus. The understanding behind these choices is that there need be no single correct interpretation. The Bible is viewed as being so inclusive that it could apply to a range of possible life situations. Therefore, we would expect a variety of interpretations to speak to a variety of life situations. Not only the Bible, but also all of its many possible interpretations, are encompassed by the expansive imagination of God. In fact, Solomon, the wisest of all humans, is reputed by the rabbis to have known three thousand stories for every verse of Scripture and one thousand and five interpretations for every story.

Learning to Tell Bible Stories

A Self-directed Workshop

1. Read the story aloud at least twice. You may choose to read the translation included here or the one you are accustomed to reading. I recommend that you examine at least two translations as you prepare, so you can hear the differences in the way they sound when read aloud.

Do read them *aloud*. Yes, if you are not by yourself, people may give you funny looks, but this really is important. Your ear will hear things about the passage that your eye will miss. Besides, you can't skim when you read aloud. You are forced to take your time, and you might notice aspects of the story that you never saw (or heard) before.

As you read, pay special attention to *where* the story takes place, *when* the story takes place, *who* the characters are, *what* objects are important to the story, and the general *order of events* in the story.

2. Now close your eyes and imagine the story taking place. This is your chance to become a playwright/director or screenwriter/filmmaker because you will experience the story on the stage or screen in your imagination. Enjoy this part of the process. It takes only a few minutes, and the budget is within everybody's reach.

3. Look back at the story briefly to make sure you haven't left out any important people, places, things, or events.

4. Try telling the story. This works better if you have someone to listen (even the family pet will do). You can try speaking aloud to yourself or to an imaginary listener. Afterwards ask your listener or yourself what questions arise as a result of this telling. Is the information you need about the people, places, things, or language in the story? Is it appropriate to the age, experiences, and interests of those who will be hearing it? Does the story capture your imagination? One more thing: You don't have to be able to explain the meaning of a story to tell it. In fact, those of the most enduring interest have an element of mystery about them.

5. Read the "Comments on the Story" that David Penchansky has provided for each passage. Are some of your questions answered there? You may wish also to look at a good Bible dictionary for place names, characters, professions, objects, or worlds that you need to learn more about. *The Interpreter's Dictionary* *of the Bible* (Nashville: Abingdon Press, 1962) is still the most complete source for storytellers.

6. Read the "Retelling the Story" section for the passage you are learning to tell. Does it give you any ideas about how you will tell the story? How would you tell it differently? Would you tell it from another character's point of view? How would that make it a different story? Would you transfer it to a modern setting? What places and characters will you choose to correspond to those in the biblical story? Remember, the retellings that are provided are not meant to be told exactly as they are written here. They are to serve as spring-boards for your imagination as you develop your telling.

7. Read the midrashim that accompany each retelling. Would you include any of these in your telling? You could introduce them by saying, "This is not in the original story, but the rabbis say. . . . " Do these midrashim respond to any of your questions or relate to any of your life situations or those of your listeners? If so, you might consider using them after the retelling to encourage persons to tell their own stories, which hearing the Bible story has brought to mind. You may even wish to begin creating some modern midrashim of your own or with your listeners.

8. Once you have gotten the elements of the story in mind and have chosen the approach you are going to take in retelling it, you need to practice, practice, practice. Tell the story aloud ten or twenty or fifty times over a period of several days or weeks. Listen as you tell your story. Revise your telling as you go along. Remember that you are not memorizing a text; you are preparing a living event. Each time you tell the story, it will be a little different, because you will be different (if for no other reason than that you have told the story before).

9. Then "taste and see" that even the stories of God are good—not all sweet, but good and good for us and for those who hunger to hear.

Ehud and King Eglon

Ehud goes on a mission to assassinate King Eglon, employing some preconceived notions about left-handed people. He accomplishes his task in one of the most graphic stories in the Bible.

The Story

Once again the Israelites did what was wrong in the eyes of the LORD, and because of this he roused King Eglon of Moab against Israel. Eglon mustered the Ammonites and the Amalekites, attacked Israel, and took possession of the city of palm trees. The Israelites were subject to King Eglon of Moab for eighteen years.

Then they cried to the LORD for help, and to deliver them he raised up Ehud son of Gera the Benjamite; he was left-handed. The Israelites sent him to hand over their tribute to King Eglon. Ehud had made himself a two-edged sword, about eighteen inches long, which he fastened on his right side under his clothes when he brought the tribute to King Eglon. Eglon was a very fat man. After Ehud had finished presenting the tribute, he sent on the men who had carried it, while he himself turned back from the Carved Stones at Gilgal. 'My lord king,' he said, 'I have a message for you in private.' Eglon called for silence and dismissed all his attendants. Ehud then approached him as he sat in the roof-chamber of his summer palace.

He said, 'Your majesty, I have a message from God for you.' As Eglon rose from his seat, Ehud reached with his left hand, drew the sword from his right side, and drove it into Eglon's belly. The hilt went in after the blade and the fat closed over the blade, for he did not draw the sword out but left it protruding behind. Ehud then went out to the porch, where he shut the door on him and fastened it.

After he had gone, Eglon's servants came and, finding the doors fastened, they said, 'He must be relieving himself in the closet of his summer place.' They waited until they became alarmed and, when he still did not open the door of the roof-chamber, they took the key and opened the door; and there was their master lying dead on the floor.

While they had been waiting, Ehud had made good his escape; he passed the Carved Stones and escaped to Seirah. Once there, he sounded the trumpet in the hill-country of Ephraim, and the Israelites went down from the hills with him at their head. He said to them, 'Follow me, for the LORD has delivered your enemies, the

23

Moabites, into your hands.' They went down after him, and held the fords of the Jordan against the Moabites, allowing no one to cross. They killed at that time some ten thousand Moabites, all of them stalwart and valiant fighters; not one escaped. Moab became subject to Israel on that day, and the land was at peace for eighty years.

Comments on the Story

Following the earliest portions of the Israelite settlement of the land of Canaan, Israel was ruled in a twofold fashion. Normal, day-to-day affairs were controlled on a tribal basis. Elders at various levels of organization were chosen by virtue of their heredity, popular choice, and advanced age. They served over the *extended family,* the smallest social unit in Israel; the *clan,* made up of a number of families; and the *tribe.* Each tribe was relatively independent, partaking with the other tribes a sense of shared history, all swearing allegiance to the same tribal God, YHWH, and recognizing to a certain extent a common priesthood.

However, there were times when the tribes needed to act in concert, functioning at a level of unity not possible under the tribal structure. At those times, it was believed that YHWH would "raise up" a leader who by virtue of supernatural empowerment would be qualified to command the absolute loyalty of two or more tribes against a common foe. These charismatic leaders, called *judges,* arose at times of national emergency. They could come from any segment of Israelite society and were believed to rule and command at the behest of YHWH. The term *judge* has little legal significance and represents more a kind of military chieftain.

Children love to tell "gross-out" stories. They tell each other the most disgusting, graphic, and degrading tales they can collect or make up. The appropriate response would be "Oh, gross!" or simply "Ooooh." The best stories would be those that forced at least one listener to run from the room with feigned or real nausea.

These stories are important in that they enable children to cope with a very frighteningly complicated adult world of requirements and obligations. By breaking the codes of decorum among themselves, children are able to cut the adult world down to a more manageable size. They know that they can never speak this way in the presence of grown-ups, and this increases the children's pleasure.

The story of how the Israelite hero Ehud outwits the overweight Moabite king Eglon is an Israelite "gross-out" story. As Israel came upon an increasingly complex international scene, it found itself all too often weak and subjugated to more powerful foreign nationalities. They told "gross-out" stories about their enemies to reduce their tension and fear, and to give vent to their hostility for nations that mistreated them.

This text is disgusting in its graphic description of viscera and excreta. This is the kind of tale that can speak to a variety of ages on a variety of levels, inspite of—or even because of—its graphic detail. I once told this story to my four-year-old son as an experiment, and as I expected, it gave him no nightmares. He asked me to repeat it many times, the "grosser" the better.

This story begins with a relationship of oppression, the Moabites against the Israelites. The Israelites are reduced to bringing valuable tribute to the excessively obese king, Eglon. His throne was on a raised dais, intricately carved with lions, bulls, or mythical animals that symbolized strength. The reader can imagine this fat king, whose soft flesh sinks in moist folds upon the cushions of his seat.

Moab had a long and troubled relationship with Israel, from the time Moab first refused to allow the escaped slaves from Egypt to cross its territory (to the south and east of Israel) on their way to possess Canaan. The two peoples understood that they were related, but Israelites told nasty stories about their Moabite ancestry (see Gen. 19:30-38). During the time before and after the monarchy, Israel and Moab constantly vied for dominance within the boundary they shared.

YHWH appointed a left-handed man, an ambiguous figure to say the least, as the one who will act on Israel's behalf. In ancient times left-handed people were considered both marginal figures, regarded with suspicion, and at the same time as magically infused individuals, looked upon with awe. Ehud the left-handed, from the tribe of Benjamin, was commissioned to break Moab's hold on Israelite territory. He devised a plan that was tailor-made for his idiosyncratic orientation. He placed a short sword on his right side (for right-handed people would always reach for a sword carried on their left side). He would likely not be frisked on the less commonly expected side, especially by the Moabites, whom the storyteller portrays as immeasurably stupid. The reader should be cautioned that this is a tale of national hostility. The Israelites, from whose perspective the story is told, are setting the Moabites up to look foolish. A similar story told in modern times would bring forth charges of racism or national chauvinism.

After bringing the tribute, Ehud returns to Eglon, the fat king, saying he carries a "secret message." The king, with dim-witted eagerness, commands a private audience with this unusual Israelite official. Ehud then pulls out the short sword from his right side and plunges it into the king's ample belly. This was his "message from God" to the king.

The wound is described in two significant ways. (Timid souls should now leave the room for a few paragraphs.) First, the fatty layer under the skin of his belly rolls up over the hilt of the short sword, compelling Ehud to leave it in the king's body. Those who discover the king would not only have difficulty finding the sword, but also they would be unable even to locate the entry wound.

Second, although short, the sword was long enough to stick out the back, and the contents of Eglon's large intestines would have emptied out all over the floor ("the dirt came out," Judg. 3:22). There is even reliable speculation that Ehud escaped through a hole in the floor that emptied into the king's personal privy. That would explain how he was able to escape unseen, while the doors to the king's chambers remained locked from the inside. Detail is piled upon disgusting detail, all contributing to Ehud's escape.

The funniest scene, although written in the characteristically sparse style of Hebrew narrative, depicts the two servants waiting outside the door to the king's private chamber. They were unwilling to disturb the king during his royal "activities." It should be obvious why they thought he was relieving himself (Judg. 3:24). A playwright of a later era might have allowed us to overhear their conversation, as they weighed the propriety of walking in on the king who (they imagined) was sitting on the toilet!

Instead, the story moves on as Ehud escapes and rallies the Israelite army to decisively defeat the demoralized and leaderless Moabite forces.

There is another story embedded in this biblical text. The ancient editor of this account, whom scholars prefer to call the Deuteronomist, has taken this old story and shaped it to meet the particular theological needs of his era. He transforms this disgusting gross-out story into a moral tale. For him, Ehud embodies the deliverance of YHWH; the Moabites exact a spiritual punishment inflicted upon the Israelites for their idolatry. Perhaps such obvious moralizing explains why we often have trouble reading this tale on its own terms. We expect it to be read through the spectacles of a moral fable instead of a gross-out joke.

The Deuteronomist accomplishes this transformation by framing the older story, giving it a new introduction and ending, leaving the middle mostly undisturbed. By shaping the story in moral and theological terms, he provides ample motivation for the Israelites, in a new and more threatening era, to preserve their religious identity against many new challenges. History, he tells us, must be understood not in terms of racial or national hostility and bias, but rather as the unfolding of God's purposes. But even more, the Deuteronomist graces us with these marvelous older stories, which he generally preserves intact.

But what can a modern storyteller do with such a story? Does it imply sanction for the assassination of heads of state? Can Ehud be identified with a modern CIA operative? Could it not rather give us insight into aspects of an ancient mentality shared by modern people as well, and by extension into the human condition? People like disgusting stories, and people like to see their enemies made to look foolish. More significant, people often respond to oppression with violence, and in ancient Israel heroes with wit enough to turn what many considered a liability into a gift were understood to be God's unique leaders.

26

Retelling the Story

"The problems in America today-YUH, are here for one-NUH and only one reason-NUH," the radio preacher hacked with utter certainty. Driving down Interstate-59 through southern Mississippi in the middle of the night left few options for any kind of broadcast sound. He much preferred music, but Joe hadn't been able to get another station more than a minute or so for the last couple of hours. Brother Buford Best's program wasn't static free, but it went on with those high-pitched sounds that hurt Joe's ears and nearly made him run off the road.

Except for the occasional truck driver whose tractor-trailer rig nearly blew his little Honda off the road, Joe Phillips was the only person headed south to New Orleans that night. It was past 2:00 A.M now, and he had a good three hours yet to go. The night was as black as could be; exits were as scarce as other signs of life. He needed the noise to keep him awake.

He hated what this old preacher was saying, but he realized that part of what was keeping him awake was his anger. Don't look a gift horse in the mouth.

The rabbis do not let the story of King Eglon stop with this sad and disgusting chapter. They say that this Moabite monarch had two daughters, one named Orpah and the other named Ruth. (*Ruth Rabbah*, 2.9)

Joe couldn't keep from talking back to Brother Buford, occasionally trying his own hand at real country preaching. "And without-TUH people like you, Brother-RUH Buford-DUH, none of us-SUH would know a thang in hell-LUH about sin-NUH. Preach on-NUH." And Brother Buford would keep at it mile after mile.

"Sufferin' is God telling people-LUH that you can't ignore his ways and get by with it-TUH!" When a nation suffers-SUH, it means that the people is payin' for their sins-SUH."

"Right, Buford," Joe spoke out, "and we won Desert Storm because we became sin free. Hallelujah!"

"Hit says right here in the Bible-LUH, Judges chapter three and verse twelve-VUH: 'And the children of Israel did evil again in the sight of the Lord-DUH: and the Lord strengthened Eglon the king of Moab against Israel-LUH, because they had done evil in the sight of the Lord-DUH.'

"God strengthened the enemy-YUH against them-MUH! They suffered because they sinned-DUH. So today-YUH, don't wonder why we got all this unemployment-TUH, politicians crookeder than a dog's hind leg-GUH, people dyin' from diseases they got from immoral sex-SUH, countries aimin' their nuclear missiles right toward your backyard-DUH. Don't wonder, I say-YUH. Don't wonder why-YUH. There's one reason-NUH and only one reason these

Sometimes even unintentional actions performed by people who are not especially religious gain God's favor. It seems that Eglon stood when he was told that Ehud had a message from God for him. Because of the unintentional homage paid to God by Eglon, he was chosen to be an ancestor of David through Ruth. (*Ruth Rabbah*, 2.9)

How did it come to pass that Naomi and Elimelech allowed their sons to marry the Moabite women, Orpah and Ruth? (See Deut. 23:3 for the prohibition of Moabites entering the assembly of the Lord.) The rabbis say that the Torah was understood by them to exclude only marriage to men from Moab, since it said Moabite and not Moabitess. (*Ruth Rabbah*, 2.9)

thangs have come to pass-SUH, and that's the sin-NUH of the American people-LUH."

"You can't believe that, you old fool!" Joe screamed. "There's plenty of sin in America, all right, but there's plenty of sin everywhere. Even in them thar ferin'-NUH countries-SUH, they got sin-NUH, Brother Buford. If God is using one country to punish another country for its collective sins, why is God using those who most defy his ways? You're crazy! Besides, people do things that are wrong without knowing that they're doing anything wrong; they sure don't mean to go against God," Joe reasoned to his radio, as he pointed to Brother Buford's voice with his right hand.

Joe slapped his radio off. He couldn't stand any more; he'd have to risk falling asleep at the wheel. He didn't know all there was to know about God by any means, but he was sure God didn't waste time trying to destroy divinely created people. Why in the world people like Brother Buford go on and on about these things in the middle of the night was beyond him. But why did so many people Joe knew believe just what Brother Buford was saying?

Deborah, the Judge and the Warrior

*The only female judge whose story appears in the Bible, Deborah wins
a battle for the Israelite general Barak. Then Jael seals the victory
when she kills the Canaanite general Sisera.*

The Story

After Ehud's death the Israelites once again did what was wrong in the eyes of the LORD, and he sold them into the power of Jabin, the Canaanite king who ruled in Hazor. The commander of his forces was Sisera, who lived in Harosheth-of-the-Gentiles. The Israelites cried to the LORD for help, because Sisera with his nine hundred iron-clad chariots had oppressed Israel harshly for twenty years.

At that time Deborah wife of Lappidoth, a prophetess, was judge in Israel. It was her custom to sit under the Palm Tree of Deborah between Ramah and Bethel in the hill-country of Ephraim, and Israelites seeking a judgment went up to her. She sent for Barak son of Abinoam from Kedesh in Naphtali and said to him, 'This is the command of the LORD the God of Israel: Go and lead out ten thousand men from Naphtali and Zebulun and bring them with you to Mount Tabor. I shall draw out to you at the wadi Kishon Jabin's commander Sisera, along with his chariots and troops, and deliver him into your power.' Barak answered, 'If you go with me, I shall go, but if you will not go, neither shall I.' 'Certainly I shall go with you,'

she said, 'but this venture will bring you no glory, because the LORD will leave Sisera to fall into the hands of a woman.' Deborah set off with Barak and went to Kedesh. . . .

. . . Deborah said to Barak, 'Up! This day the LORD is to give Sisera into your hands. See, the LORD has marched out at your head!' Barak came down from Mount Tabor with ten thousand men at his back, and the LORD threw Sisera and all his chariots and army into panic-stricken rout before Barak's onslaught; Sisera himself dismounted from his chariot and fled on foot. Barak pursued the chariots and the troops as far as Harosheth, and the whole army was put to the sword; not a man was left alive.

Meanwhile Sisera fled on foot to the tent of Jael wife of Heber the Kenite, because King Jabin of Hazor and the household of Heber the Kenite were on friendly terms. Jael came out to greet Sisera and said, 'Come in, my lord, come in here; do not be afraid.' He went into the tent, and she covered him with a rug. He said to her, 'Give me some water to drink, for I am thirsty.' She opened a skin of milk,

29

gave him a drink, and covered him again. He said to her, 'Stand at the tent door, and if anyone comes and asks if there is a man here, say "No."' But as Sisera lay fast asleep through exhaustion Jael took a tent-peg, picked up a mallet, and, creeping up to him, drove the peg into his temple, so that it went down into the ground, and Sisera died. When Barak came by in pursuit of Sisera, Jael went out to meet him, 'Come,' she said, 'I shall show you the man you are looking for.' He went in with her, and there was Sisera lying dead with the tent-peg in his temple. That day God gave victory to the Israelites over King Jabin of Canaan, and they pressed home their attacks upon him until he was destroyed.

Comments on the Story

This story begins with a standard conflict between prophet and government, similar to the story of Isaiah and Ahaz (Isa. 7). In that narrative, Isaiah challenges King Ahaz to ask for a sign, and Ahaz refuses, saying he does not want to test God. The king is punished and publicly rebuked for his lack of faith. Deborah is more like these later prophetic figures who maintained an advisory capacity with the administrative/military leaders. She did not rule militarily, as did the earlier, spirit-empowered figures we find in Judges.

And she was a woman. In the ancient world women were second-class citizens at best; at worst, property of their husbands and fathers. This woman, serving as legal authority and spiritual elder of the tribes, is highly unusual, and her status speaks of the willingness of Israel to accept any person they perceived to be chosen by YHWH.

She tells General Barak to fight a battle against the formidable forces of Sisera, the Canaanite general who commanded a division of iron-banded chariots, the latest technology in military hardware. Barak refuses to go into battle unless Deborah accompanies him. He has no confidence that the presence of YHWH will stay with him, if she is not present. She consents, but pronounces that he will not get glory from the victory (an important issue for men), but that it will go to a woman; whether the woman was Deborah herself or Jael later in the story is not clear—probably both. Why would Barak agree to such an arrangement? It is unlikely that Barak was indifferent to his reputation, but his fear of defeat or abandonment by YHWH outweighed all other considerations.

Deborah accompanies Barak into the battle, and YHWH neutralizes the military advantage of the Canaanites. We are fortunate to have this story in two forms, a prose form in chapter 4 and a poetic version in chapter 5. The poem of Israel's victory is thought to be one of the oldest texts in the Bible, much older than the prose account. Ancient storytellers usually recounted the mighty acts of their heroes in poetry, but in modern times, we tell stories in prose form. Poetry captures the emotional intensity of an action, being by nature more compressed than prose. It can simply be read out loud, or more effectively a homily can present an audience with a few salient points from the poem, brought out through the eyes of the storyteller.

For instance, the straightforward narrative does not give specific information as to exactly how the chariots were neutralized. "And [YHWH] threw Sisera and all his chariots and army into panic-stricken rout before Barak's onslaught" (Judg. 4:15). But the poem is more informative:

> "[YHWH,] when you went out from Seir,
>   when you marched from the region of Edom,
> the earth trembled,
>   and the heavens poured
>   the clouds indeed poured water.
> The mountains quaked before
>   [YHWH], the One of Sinai,
>   before [YHWH], the God of Israel."
>
> (Judges 5:4-5)

The poem speaks of a giant, sudden thunderstorm that rendered the plain muddy. The wheels of Sisera's iron chariots stuck. The poet identifies YHWH with this powerful storm, which comes up from the south. The weather is often a great leveler in many contests.

Sisera, the enemy, was compelled to flee on foot. He came upon a desert settlement. A woman let him into her home, and he immediately began ordering her around. "Hide me. Give me a drink. Stand by the door of the tent and say . . . " Obviously Sisera was accustomed to giving orders and being obeyed unquestionably, particularly by a woman.

His recent military defeat and the loss of his entire army must have weighed very heavily on him. She ministers to his needs, and he soon falls asleep. How exhausted he must have been, physically and emotionally. The crude tent, made of woven goat skin faded from the sun, provided him with relief and shelter.

This woman, Jael, had strong, thick arms from her life of hard work, the heavy lifting and carrying required to maintain her life in a nomadic community. While he slept, she took a heavy, wooden tent peg and mallet and pinned Sisera's skull to the floor of the tent.

Through slow-motion repetition (which is a technique the storyteller might employ), the poem paints a more horrible picture—in it, he was still standing.

> She put her hand to the tent peg
>   and her right hand to the workmen's mallet;
> she struck Sisera a blow,
>   she crushed his head,
>   she shattered and pierced his temple.

31

He sank, he fell,
  he lay still at her feet;
at her feet he sank, he fell;
  where he sank, there he fell dead.
                              (Judges 5:26-27)

So Barak lost the glory of victory twice, once when Deborah accompanied him into battle, and second when Jael destroyed his enemy. For that matter, YHWH didn't give him much opportunity to show off his military prowess in the actual battle, which was decided by a fortuitous thunderstorm.

But the most poignant scene occurs at the end of the poem. This ancient poet wants to communicate how absolute was the Israelite victory by depicting not only the loss of life on the battlefield, but also the onrushing despair back in the walled city, where the women waited eagerly for their men to return with their lives and with the spoils of war.

Out of the window she peered,
  the mother of Sisera gazed
    through the lattice:
"Why is his chariot so long in coming?
  Why tarry the hoofbeats of his chariots?"
Her wisest ladies make answer,
  indeed, she answers the question herself:
"Are they not finding and dividing the spoil?—
  A girl or two for every man;
spoil of dyed stuffs for Sisera,
  spoil of dyed stuffs embroidered,
  two pieces of dyed work
    embroidered for my neck as spoil?"
                              (Judges 5:28-30)

We readers know what she doesn't—that her son will never return. He lies dead in a pool of blood on the floor of Jael's tent. Sisera's mother joins the vast company of bereaved families awaiting their loved ones' return from war—and they never return.

The kind of power the women in the story wield is terrifying: to declare war and lead into battle, to kill someone violently, when first offering hospitality and then betraying a very sacred obligation to welcome the stranger.

Some have said that when women move into roles of leadership, power will be wielded differently, but it is difficult to discern the difference in the histories of modern India, Israel, Britain, Pakistan, and the Philippines, where women have held power. It might be helpful in developing the biblical narrative to tell the story from Barak's perspective—the prototypical "second banana"—or from Jael's—the woman warrior—or perhaps from the perspective of the great military leader who fell from power, the formerly great Sisera, helpless at the hands of a determined woman.

Retelling the Story

"We brought you to this campus to help us expand our course offerings and, thereby, appeal to a wider student population," the college president said with an edge to his voice. "You and I both know, Dean Drummond, that in the five years you have been here, enrollment has continued to decline. And our students look about like they've always looked. We're not reaching new people, and the trustees are giving us a year—one more year—to begin to regain some of our losses. Otherwise, one or both of us will be looking for a new job!"

"Dr. Greg," the dean whined, "I don't know what else to do. I've increased teaching loads and pushed

In many midrashim Sisera is portrayed as a gigantic and powerful figure. It was said that his shout could destroy a city's walls and freeze the wildest of beasts in fear. It took nine hundred horses to pull his chariot, and when he went for a swim the fish that were trapped in his beard would feed a host of famished eaters. The fearsome general was said to have conquered the entire known world by the time he turned thirty years old. All this, and he was defeated by a woman. (Ginzberg IV, p. 35)

the whole staff as far as I think I can. I've brought in the best consulting firms I could find. We've had evaluations of our present programs by every group on campus: the administration, the faculty, and the students themselves. I've tried to implement all reasonable suggestions, and nothing has changed. No one is more frustrated than I. I've come to the conclusion that the problem is the time in which we live and the economy over which none of us has any control."

"Well we'd better find a way to control it, Lloyd, or else the economy will become a very personal concern, if you know what I mean."

Dean Lloyd Drummond left the president's office, enraged that anyone with *his* impeccable academic credentials had to tolerate the rantings of someone intellectually inferior to himself and who, worst of all, viewed the college purely from a standpoint of dollars and cents. Even Greg wasn't exactly setting the woods on fire as a college president, Drummond thought.

Drummond ordered his secretary to call an emergency meeting of all department chairs the next morning at 7:00; no absences would be tolerated. He would place the blame for this problem on the shoulders of those more responsible for it, those who had more dealings with the students. Dean Drummond left the campus that day in a huff, but he was determined to forget the whole affair by the time he sat down to dinner.

Deborah was a judge among the people. Since it was considered inappropriate for men to visit a woman in her house, Deborah set up her court outdoors. This was perhaps the first judicial system with public access to trials. She and her husband also made candles for God's sanctuary. It is told that Deborah always made hers with thick wicks so they would burn brightly and their light would last a long time. So God proclaimed that, since Deborah had taken such pains to bring light to the house of worship, her light would shine throughout the entire land. She served as judge for forty years, and at her death the entire nation mourned for seventy days and the land was at peace for seven years.
(Ginzberg IV, pp. 35-39)

President Greg was the last administrator to leave the main building—as usual. "How are you, sir?" asked Estelle, the maid who cleaned up the president's office.

"Not very well, Estelle, not very well."

"I'm sorry to hear that, Doctor Greg."

"If we don't reach more students, Estelle, I'm not sure any of us will be around here in two years."

"That's awful news—just awful. I sure hate to hear it. If you all had classes at this time of day, I'd make one more student than what we got now. I've been wanting to study history, but there's no time."

"Well, I do appreciate your sentiment, Estelle. Have a good evening. I have to run now. If I'm late for dinner again, Mrs. Greg will never let me hear the end of it!"

The next morning, the department chairs were leaving their meeting with Dean Drummond—some with flushed faces, others rolling their eyes back into their heads. Once again, the dean had tried to make them the scapegoats for his own lack of creativity and vision in the face of crisis. Drummond, feeling good about placing responsibility where it needed to be, answered a call from the president's secretary; he was needed at once in the president's office.

"Lloyd, I've come across the solution to our problem."

"What is it, Evan?"

"We need to offer classes when people who work and are tied up during the day can take them. We need night classes; maybe some on the weekends too."

"That'll never work here. Nothing in all our surveys even suggests this possibility. Besides, none of our 'star' professors want to teach those hours."

"Have you asked them?"

"I have a feel for these things, you know. Well, maybe we don't have to use our big names at those hours; or if we do, we won't make it a matter of choice."

"It's not a matter of choice, Dean Drummond. Implement this effective next semester!"

"May I ask where you came across this idea?"

"Absolutely. Estelle gave me the idea."

"Estelle who? The only Estelle on our staff is . . . You have to be kidding!"

Bringing up student enrollment and strengthening the college's financial position didn't happen instantly, but, in time, the college flourished.

Jael put on her best clothes and most expensive jewelry to lure Sisera to her bed. Her voice, whispered and husky, was as attractive as her appearance. She prepared a comfortable place for the general to sleep and placed fresh, fragrant roses all around it. She brought goat milk and wine mixed with water to Sisera. Just as she suspected, as the general began to become tipsy he made a pass at her. The rabbis disagree on what happened next. Some say that Jael gave in to Sisera's passionate advances in order to get close enough to kill him. Others say she refused his overtures and simply waited for him to fall asleep before she struck. In any case, after she had driven the wooden spike through his skull she is reported to have said, "Now go to your dead and tell them that their great and mighty general was conquered by the hand of a woman." (Ginzberg IV, p. 37 and VI, p. 198)

It is interesting to note that Deuteronomy 22:5 is sometimes interpreted to mean that women are prohibited from using weapons. This is the reason offered by some rabbis that Jael uses a hammer and spike rather than Sisera's own weapons of war.

Gideon

Gideon puts God to the test, then after he has won a battle in the most unlikely way refuses to become king because only YHWH can rule Israel.

The Story

The angel of the LORD came to Ophrah and sat under the terebinth which belonged to Joash the Abiezrite. While Gideon son of Joash was threshing wheat in the winepress, so that he might keep it out of sight of the Midianites, the angel of the LORD appeared to him and said, 'You are a brave man, and the LORD is with you.' 'Pray, my lord,' said Gideon, 'if the LORD really is with us, why has all this happened to us? What has become of all those wonderful deeds of his, of which we have heard from our forefathers, when they told us how the LORD brought us up from Egypt? But now the LORD has cast us off and delivered us into the power of the Midianites.'

The LORD turned to him and said, 'Go and use this strength of yours to free Israel from the Midianites. It is I who send you.' Gideon said, 'Pray, my lord, how can I save Israel? Look at my clan: it is the weakest in Manasseh, and I am the least in my father's family.' The LORD answered, 'I shall be with you, and you will lay low all Midian as one man.' He replied, 'If I stand so well with you, give me a sign that it is you who speak to me. Do not leave this place, I beg you,

until I come with my gift and lay it before you.' He answered, 'I shall stay until you return.' . . .

Gideon said to God, 'If indeed you are going to deliver Israel through me as you promised, I shall put a fleece of wool on the threshing-floor, and if there is dew on the fleece while all the ground is dry, then I shall be sure that it is through me you will deliver Israel as you promised.' And that is what happened. When he rose early next day and wrung out the fleece, he squeezed enough dew from it to fill a bowl with water. Gideon then said to God, 'Do not be angry with me, but give me leave to speak once again. Allow me, I pray, to make one more test with the fleece. This time let the fleece be dry, and all the ground be covered with dew.' God let it be so that night: the fleece alone was dry, and all over the ground there was dew. . . .

Gideon sent all these Israelites home, but he kept the three hundred, and they took with them the jars and the trumpets which the people had.

The Midianite camp was below him in the valley, and that night the LORD said to Gideon, 'Go down at once and attack the camp, for I have delivered

36

it into your hands. If you are afraid to do so, then go down first with your servant Purah, and when you hear what they are saying, that will give you courage to attack the camp.' So he and his servant Purah went down to the outposts of the camp where the fighting men were stationed. The Midianites, the Amalekites, and all the eastern tribes were so many that they lay there in the valley like a swarm of locusts; there was no counting their camels, which in number were like grains of sand on the seashore. As Gideon came close, there was a man telling his comrades about a dream. He said, 'I dreamt that I saw a barley loaf rolling over and over through the Midianite camp; it came to a tent, struck it, and the tent collapsed and turned upside down.' The other answered, 'This can be none other than the sword of Gideon son of Joash the Israelite. God has delivered Midian and the whole army into his hands.'

When Gideon heard the account of the dream and its interpretation, he bowed down in worship. Then going back to the Israelite camp he said, 'Let us go! The LORD has delivered the camp of the Midianites into our hands.' He divided the three hundred men into three companies, and furnished every man with a trumpet and an empty jar, with a torch inside each jar. 'Watch me,' he said to them. 'When I come to the edge of the camp, do exactly as I do. When I and those with me blow our trumpets, you too all round the camp blow your trumpets and shout, "For the LORD and for Gideon!"'

Gideon and the hundred men who were with him reached the outskirts of the camp at the beginning of the middle watch, just after the posting of the sentries. They blew the trumpets and smashed the jars they were holding. All three companies blew their trumpets and smashed their jars; then, grasping the torches in their left hands and the trumpets in their right, they shouted, 'A sword for the LORD and for Gideon!' Every man stood where he was, all round the camp, and the whole camp leapt up in a panic and took flight. When the three hundred blew their trumpets, the LORD set all the men in the camp fighting against each other. . . .

The Israelites said to Gideon, 'You have saved us from the Midianites; now you be our ruler, you and your son and your grandson.' But Gideon replied, 'I shall not rule over you, nor will my son; the LORD will rule over you.' He went on, 'I have a request to make: will every one of you give me an ear-ring from his booty?'—for the enemy, being Ishmaelites, wore gold ear-rings. They said, 'Of course we shall give them.' So a cloak was spread out and every man threw on to it a gold ear-ring from his booty. The ear-rings he asked for weighed seventeen hundred shekels of gold; this was in addition to the crescents and pendants and the purple robes worn by the Midianite kings, and not counting the chains on the necks of their camels. Gideon made the gold into an ephod which he set up in his own town of Ophrah. All the Israelites went astray by worshipping it, and it became a snare for Gideon and his household.

Thus the Midianites were subdued by the Israelites; they could no longer hold up their heads. For forty years the land was at peace, all the lifetime of Gideon.

Comments on the Story

Gideon, an Israelite from an obscure Israelite tribe, doubted God. When the angel blessed him, "YHWH is with you, brave man, hero of Israel," Gideon responded, "Where is this ancestral god? I've heard stories about him, but see no evidence."

There is a tone of suspicion in Gideon's voice, as if he were afraid that the angel's confident pronouncement is not exactly reliable. He doesn't even believe that the ancestral stories, comforting as they are, ever really happened. Gideon's tone gives the sense that for his community the entire foundation of Israelite confidence is collapsing. For Gideon, these stories of YHWH no longer work.

The Midianites, a desert tribe, had overrun the land of Israel. This gang of bandits enslaved the Israelites when they could and stole from them otherwise. The Israelites found it necessary to bring their grain (in concealment) to wine presses. They threshed the sheaves, while watching nervously for Midianites who would readily steal their sustenance, thereby allowing Israelite families to starve. The Midianites returned Israelite clans to slave or refugee status.

This injustice was quite a blow for a people who generally believed that the supreme God was their advocate against the other tribes and nations. Continuous defeats and humiliation struck them to the core of their faith.

No wonder Gideon initiated tests to make sure that YHWH, the Israelite God, was adequate for the task of delivering Israel. Gideon tested YHWH in two ways. First, Gideon wanted to see whether YHWH could manipulate nature. In certain seasons, the ground is soaked every morning with dew. Gideon dared YHWH to make the dew fall only on a fleece laid on the ground, while the rest of the ground remained dry.

When YHWH performed this miracle, Gideon demanded another test—this time wet the ground but keep the fleece dry, and it was so, the very next day.

Gideon has earned a reputation among interpreters for being unreasonable in his dealings with YHWH, but Israel's primary heroes are often characterized with this annoying persistence and mistrust. For instance, Abraham argued with YHWH concerning the cities of the plain, Sodom and Gomorrah. Jeremiah and Habakkuk disputed with God concerning divine justice; not to mention the chief figures among doubters, Job and Qoheleth (Ecclesiastes). Such assertiveness and questioning was greatly appreciated among some segments of Israelite society, especially the sages. Doubt, often seen by modern religious people as the enemy of faith, was seen by these teachers in Israel as an essential element of religious commitment. The storyteller might focus on the way our testing God often turns into God's test of our faithfulness.

A good example of such a turn around is the next scene, in which it is not clear who is testing whom. Gideon is compelled by YHWH to keep reducing the number of his troops. First he releases all who wish they weren't there; those who were afraid to fight. Out of thirty-two thousand troops, only ten thousand remain. Then YHWH instructs Gideon to watch the men drink at a stream. Those who bent down and slurped water like dogs were eliminated. Only those who remained watchful for adversaries, cupping the water in their hands and bringing it to their mouths, would fight the Midianites. That left only three hundred warriors out of an original thirty-two thousand. Only then was YHWH ready to direct the battle.

There has been a lot of discussion of unilateral disarmament in recent years, but Gideon's action is absurd. Would any general in a reasonable state of mind willingly give the enemy so dramatic an advantage on the very eve of battle? That is exactly what Gideon did.

So Gideon shrewdly asked for a third test. This test was different. Before trying to fight with an army of only three hundred men, he wanted proof that he would win the next day's battle. YHWH transported him to witness a conversation between soldiers in the enemy camp. They were discussing a dream:

"A cake of barley bread tumbled into the camp of Midian, and came to the tent, and struck it so that it fell; it turned upside down, and the tent collapsed." And his comrade answered, "This is no other than the sword of Gideon . . . into his hand God has given Midian and all the army." (Judges 7:13)

Interestingly enough, the war was won, not with miracles but with Gideon's wit and stealth; less with violence, and more by an act of theater. The three hundred soldiers held lit torches under clay jars, and at a given signal they broke the jars and shouted "The sword of YHWH and Gideon."

The Midianites woke to the loud, clattering sound of three hundred pots breaking at once and the smell of burning. They left their tents and found themselves surrounded by lit torches, all in motion; they believed that each torch guided an entire platoon of night fighters. The Midianites perceived themselves to be badly outnumbered and began to strike out in the darkness against each other in their confusion, adding to the noise. In the midst of the grunts, the clatter of sword against sword, and painful screams, the battle became a complete rout.

In our complex world of technological advancement, with weapons of mass destruction, it is hard to imagine a just war, but the storyteller here clearly admires Gideon, the doubter, the hard bargainer, who obtained freedom for a nation armed primarily with imagination. The angel's blessing at the beginning became a challenge; YHWH placed Gideon at the very edge of what was possible, and Gideon did great things.

Gideon makes two more decisions, one good and one bad, which leaves us with mixed feelings about his leadership. This should not be surprising, since we often have such mixed feelings about our leaders. It simply underscores Gideon's very human character. His weaknesses are our weaknesses.

The elders of his tribe (and perhaps representatives from some other tribes) requested that he "rule" over them. By not using the word *king (melek)*, they were trying to avoid a controversial subject, since no king had ever ruled Israel. This is, in fact, chronologically the first mention in the Bible of a *melek* as leader in Israel. But to make it clear exactly what they wanted, they further specified, "Your son, and your grandson also." They were asking for the establishment of a kingly dynasty—no ambiguity here.

Gideon refused. They wounded his honor by suggesting such a thing. "I will not rule over you, and my son will not rule over you; [YHWH] will rule over you" (Judg. 8:23). Gideon wanted to share the glory of battle with YHWH, but he had no desire to compete with YHWH as absolute ruler.

"Oh, and one more thing," Gideon adds. "Give me some of the gold you stole from the Midianite army." They piled it on a blanket, assembling a sizable fortune. With it, Gideon cast a golden ephod. We have little idea of what an ephod was in this context. Usually it is a kind of tunic worn under the priest's ceremonial clothes, sometimes a ceremonial vest, or perhaps a general word for this undergarment, but we do not know enough to imagine the Israelites worshiping a vest, even one made of gold. Did they believe YHWH wore it? In any case, this ephod was idolatrous, and it "snared" them; that is, it drew them into religious impurity and unfaithfulness to God. Once again they worshiped a thing they could see instead of the invisible YHWH.

So Gideon, in spite of his intelligence, his humility, and even his great faith in the midst of doubt, finally leaves us with this bittersweet impression of one who refused the idolatry of kingship but encouraged the idolatry of a golden shrine. Even in our time all too often a political leader will sacrifice for the sake of public service, and then feel that the public owes him or her some perk that the politician is perfectly justified in appropriating, even if it bends the rules a bit.

Retelling the Story

Gideon was a bottom-line kind of guy, and, what was more, he was a skeptic. Some people claimed everything that crossed their minds was a message from God; Gideon didn't trust himself or human nature enough to be so all fired sure of that. As a result, he had gotten into the habit of testing rather carefully any word he believed he was getting from on high.

Those who knew General Gideon well enough to see what went on between him and God wondered whether God got tired of giving Gideon extra encouragement and extra signs. Wasn't it sufficient for God or God's angel to say things one time? Yet, no matter how much his friends and associates warned him, Gideon went right on with his verification process in regard to divine messages. It all began when he was just a lad.

"Yeah. Right," Gideon said to a big oak tree one day while he and members of his family were trying to thresh wheat out of the sight of any Midianites.

"I didn't say anything to you, Gideon," said his father, Joash.

"I wasn't talking to you either," explained Gideon. "I was talking to that angel over there."

"Well, give him my regards, son, and then get on with your work. The Midianites could come upon us any time. We must hurry!"

"I know that, Dad. I didn't invite the angel here. I'm minding my own business when I look up, and there he is. Have you ever tried ignoring an angel?"

Joash shook his head and went on with his work.

"The Lord God is with *me?*" Gideon asked the angel at the oak tree. "Well he has a funny way of showing it. God did great things for our ancestors all right, but the Midianites are starving us to death; and we've not seen hide or hair of God."

"Gideon," Joash began to speak.

"Please, Dad, I can't hear him if you talk, too."

There was a pause while Gideon listened before speaking to the angel of the Lord. "Our little clan can't take down the Midianites! There's no way. We're one of the smallest and weakest groups in Manesseh. In my own family, I am the least. You must have me mixed up with someone else."

The rabbis say that Gideon was chosen by God for his particular role in saving the people not because he was especially brave but because he had been a good son to his father. When his father was old and fearful that the Midianites would attack and kill such an aged prey to get his grain, Gideon told his father to go home. "If the Midianites come after me, I am fast enough to run away." It is interesting that he did not say that he would stay and give his life for his father's grain. Perhaps in Gideon God had found a leader who truly believed that "discretion is the better part of valor." (Ginzberg IV, pp. 40-41)

Gideon justified asking God for a sign because Moses had first asked for a sign when God had appeared to him in the voice from the burning bush. When Gideon asked the angel for a sign, God's messenger told him to pour water over a stone. When Gideon did this, half of the water turned to blood and half turned to fire. Even so, the blood did not put out the fire, nor did the fire dry up the blood. Thus Gideon knew that this was truly a sign from God. (Ginzberg IV, p. 40)

After Gideon's death the people worshiped the ephod he had commanded to be made. The rabbis say that people of that time used to carry around small carved figures of the god Beelzebub with them. Some would even take these tiny idols out and kiss them for luck or for good fortune or just to be sure all their bases were covered. This is why they were so quick to idolize Gideon's ephod. (Ginzberg IV, p. 41)

Another pause. "All right, then," Gideon insisted, "if God has so much confidence in me, I want a sign that you're real and not just the hot sun beating down on my head."

The hospitable thing to do was to provide a meal for a guest, so Gideon asked the angel to wait while he took care of this matter. The angel agreed to linger. In a while, Gideon set before the angel a nice lunch, but the angel told him to put the food on a rock and to dump the broth. Gideon did so, wishing he hadn't gone to so much trouble, and when he did, fire appeared as if out of the rock and burnt the bread and meat to a crisp. Gideon rubbed his eyes in disbelief, and at once the angel disappeared. Gideon still couldn't see himself as a military man, but he knew then that God had been in this visitation and that he must do what the angel told him.

42

Samson

Samson is a judge with a weakness for foreign women, and he seems to be as gullible as he is strong. In the end he is remembered not for his strength or his failures, but simply as one who chose to do the divine bidding.

The Story

Samson went to Gaza, and seeing a prostitute there he lay with her. The people of Gaza heard that Samson had come, and they gathered round and lay in wait for him all night at the city gate. During the night, however, they took no action, saying to themselves, 'When dawn comes we shall kill him.' Samson stayed in bed till midnight; but then he rose, took hold of the doors of the city gate and the two gateposts, and pulled them out, bar and all; he hoisted them on his shoulders, and carried them to the top of the hill east of Hebron.

Afterwards Samson fell in love with a woman named Delilah, who lived by the wadi of Sorek. The lords of the Philistines went up to her and said, 'Cajole him and find out what gives him his great strength, and how we can overpower and bind him and render him helpless. We shall each give you eleven hundred pieces of silver.'

Delilah said to Samson, 'Tell me, what gives you your great strength? How could you be bound and made helpless?' 'If I were bound with seven fresh bowstrings not yet dry,' replied Samson, 'then I should become no stronger than any other man.' The

lords of the Philistines brought her seven fresh bowstrings not yet dry, and she bound him with them. She had men concealed in the inner room, and she cried, 'Samson, the Philistines are upon you!' Thereupon he snapped the bowstrings as a strand of tow snaps at the touch of fire, and his strength was not impaired.

Delilah said to Samson, 'You have made a fool of me and lied to me. Now tell me this time how you can be bound.' He said to her, 'If I were tightly bound with new ropes that have never been used, then I should become no stronger than any other man.' Delilah took new ropes and bound him with them. Then, with men concealed in the inner room, she cried, 'Samson, the Philistines are upon you!' But he snapped the ropes off his arms like thread.

Delilah said to him, 'You are still making a fool of me, still lying to me. Tell me: how can you be bound?' He said, 'Take the seven loose locks of my hair, weave them into the warp, and drive them tight with the beater; then I shall become no stronger than any other man.' So she lulled him to sleep, wove the seven loose locks of

43

his hair into the warp, drove them tighter with the beater, and cried, 'Samson, the Philistines are upon you!' He woke from sleep and pulled away the warp and the loom with it.

She said to him, 'How can you say you love me when you do not confide in me? This is the third time you have made a fool of me and have not told me what gives you your great strength.' She so pestered him with these words day after day, pressing him hard and wearying him to death, that he told her the whole secret. 'No razor has touched my head,' he said, 'because I am a Nazirite, consecrated to God from the day of my birth. If my head were shaved, then my strength would leave me, and I should become no stronger than any other man.'

Delilah realized that he had told her his secret, and she sent word to the lords of the Philistines: 'Come up at once,' she said; 'he has told me his secret.' The lords of the Philistines came, bringing the money with them. She lulled Samson to sleep on her lap, and then summoned a man to shave the seven locks of his hair. She was now making him helpless. When his strength had left him, she cried, 'Samson, the Philistines are upon you!' He woke from his sleep and thought, 'I will go out as usual and shake myself'; he did not know that the LORD had left him. Then the Philistines seized him, gouged out his eyes, and brought him down to Gaza. There they bound him with bronze fetters, and he was set to grinding grain in the prison. But his hair, after it had been shaved, began to grow again.

The lords of the Philistines assembled to offer a great sacrifice to their god Dagon, and to rejoice and say,

'Our god has delivered into our hands
Samson our enemy.'

The people, when they saw him, praised their god, chanting:

'Our god has delivered our enemy into our hands,
the scourge of our land who piled it with our dead.'

When they grew merry, they said, 'Call Samson, and let him entertain us.' When Samson was summoned from prison, he was a source of entertainment to them. They then stood him between the pillars, and Samson said to the boy who led him by the hand, 'Put me where I can feel the pillars which support the temple, so that I may lean against them.' The temple was full of men and women, and all the lords of the Philistines were there, and there were about three thousand men and women on the roof watching the entertainment.

Samson cried to the LORD and said, 'Remember me, Lord GOD, remember me: for this one occasion, God, give me strength, and let me at one stroke be avenged on the Philistines for my two eyes.' He put his arms round the two central pillars which supported the temple, his right arm round one and his left round the other and, bracing himself, he said, 'Let me die with the Philistines.' Then Samson leaned forward with all his might, and the temple crashed down on the lords and all the people who were in it. So the dead whom he killed at his death were more than those he had killed in his life.

His brothers and all his father's family came down, carried him up to the grave of his father Manoah between Zorah and Eshtaol, and buried him there. He had been judge over Israel for twenty years.

44

Comments on the Story

Samson must have been the most foolish champion Israel ever had. This most famous story about Samson pictures him lying in the arms of his lover. The Philistines had paid her to extract the secret of Samson's strength. She asks him, and in a stereotypical portrayal of a nagging, petulant woman, she whines until he gives her an answer. "How can you say, 'I love you,' when your heart is not with me? You have mocked me three times now and have not told me what makes your strength so great" (Judg. 16:15).

He dreams up a hare-brained explanation for his superhuman strength and says that seven bowstrings will hold him. So Delilah ties him with seven new bowstrings and tells him that the Philistines are coming. He wakes and finds himself bound, but shakes the thin restraints. He then notices the bedroom full of embarrassed Philistines in full battle gear, excusing themselves and filing out of the room. A man of greater discernment might have asked "Why were all those Philistines hidden in our bedroom?" but Samson just nestles back in Delilah's lap. She cries again that he doesn't love her because he lied to her. The bowstrings lie broken on the floor, mute reminders of her treachery.

A second time Samson concocts an explanation for his strength, to turn aside her incessant questioning. If he is tied with an unused rope, he tells his Philistine lover, he will be helpless "like anyone else" (Judg. 16:11) Again, Samson is awakened, again the ropes snap like threads, and he finds a room full of embarrassed Philistines leaving his presence, their swords held awkwardly at their sides.

Samson, foolishly smitten with this Philistine woman, nestles back into Delilah's lap as she scolds him for lying to her a second time. But now he spins a tale a little closer to the truth. If she weaves his hair into a loom it will rob him of his strength. Again the alarm, again the broken restraint, and again the sheepish Philistines smiling awkwardly as they flee Samson's anger. Most people would have caught on by now, but not Samson.

Finally, in exasperation, he tells her the truth. If his head is shaved, it will break his special relationship with YHWH and place Samson at the mercy of his enemies. Delilah, of course, calls the barber as soon as Samson drifts off. This time when he awakens, the Philistines grab him, blind him by gouging out his eyes, and drag him away.

This kind of repetition in storytelling builds tension and intensifies the resolution. When we were children, all our favorite stories employed this style of repetition—"Goldilocks and the Three Bears," "The Three Little Pigs," and "Little Red Riding Hood," for instance. Such repetition characterizes oral narratives across the ages and the world.

But this is only part of a longer story of Samson. Unfortunately, despite additional evidence our evaluation of his character remains unchanged.

We first meet a grown Samson in chapter 14, insisting that his parents "get" for him a particular Philistine woman who had aroused him. Like a spoiled child, Samson knows nothing of deferring his appetites, insisting that what attracts him at the moment must be his. His hapless parents plead with him, but ultimately do what he wishes.

His mother and father argue from a perspective of narrow-minded ethnocentrism: "Isn't there a nice Israelite girl who attracts you? Why go to the Philistines?" After all, the Philistines had invaded and occupied increasing tracts of Israelite territory as they moved relentlessly eastward, expanding from their coastal settlements. It is possible that true love could have blossomed between this young man and a woman from a hostile culture, as in a "Romeo and Juliet" story. However, this is unlikely, because Samson is painted with the less than flattering tones of religious unfaithfulness and unbridled appetite. What stands out in this episode is Samson's childish insistence, "But I want this one!" Like a child begging for a toy, he wears down his parents' resistance, as Delilah wore down his later in life.

At this point in the narrative, the author feels that it is necessary to remind the hearer that Samson is a hero of Israel's past and not a petulant child, and asserts that YHWH is behind Samson's demand so as to seek an occasion against Philistia. What can this mean? Did YHWH inspire Samson to act like a brat, a lustful martinet, so as to put him in a situation where he loses his temper and slaughters innocent Philistine civilians? Or is the writer simply asserting that YHWH can employ even the worst of human traits in a divine scheme. The text never resolves this tension between Samson the brat and Samson the charismatic hero of YHWH.

This story seems to function to undercut the whole charismatic ideal of early Israelite leadership. The writer reminds us that a figure might be anointed by YHWH, might win great victories over Israel's enemies, but still be inwardly corrupt and ultimately destructive to Israel's fortunes. The writer is hinting that only by instituting a monarchy—a professional, full-time administrative branch of government—can this inner rot among Israel's heroes be eliminated. In this sense the story argues for the superiority of a later form of leadership.

Samson challenges his Philistine wedding party to answer a riddle. He bets them sixty garments, and they pressure his bride to worm the answer out of Samson. She is only the first Philistine woman to get her way with Samson through dogged persistence. Delilah will appear on the scene later. When Samson is bested, his language turns sexually crude and abusive: "If you had not plowed with my heifer, you would not have found out my riddle" (Judg. 14:18). Then he murders thirty Philistine men to obtain the garments he owes. The narrator tells us that he does this because the "Spirit of YHWH comes upon him."

The murder and mayhem do not stop there. Samson's wife is given to another. When he finds out, he destroys all the crops and olive trees in her town. When the community burns alive his bride and her father in an act of revenge, the narrator describes Samson's response by saying he "struck them down hip and thigh with great slaughter" (Judg. 15:8). And on and on the cycle of violence goes.

Finally, at the end of his life, Samson is blinded, bound to a millstone to grind grain like a beast of burden. "But the hair of his head began to grow again" (Judg. 16:22). The listener remembers that Samson's hair is the sign of his strength and so is in on a secret that even Samson's taskmasters may not know. He asks for strength one last time to avenge the Philistines for the loss of his eyes. He pulls down their temple while three thousand Philistines are inside. The narrator writes this sad and gruesome epitaph. "So those he killed at his death were more than those he had killed during his life" (Judg. 16:30).

What shall we do with this man, this killer of Philistines, who is ruled by passion, anger, and lust? The narrator tells us that the Spirit of YHWH inspired him in much that he did. How can this be?

This is a tough story, especially tough if one makes the effort to glean some spiritual truth from its twists and turns. The following suggestions might be useful to the storyteller.

An influential idea in Israel asserted that YHWH favored Israel unconditionally. The writer of the Samson story may be suggesting that Samson's life is a parable of Israel. The hero was anointed by God but was ruined through uncontrolled passions; Israel's religious unfaithfulness is often compared to sexual unfaithfulness.

Certainly the Samson story is not isolated as a tale of a hero with feet of clay. Biblical storytellers are able to look at both the gifts and the defects of their leaders, heroes, or kings without flinching. Israelite literature commonly depicts its heroes as less than exemplary figures, partly to demonstrate the unique activity of YHWH on their behalf. One has only to consider Jacob's dishonesty, Joseph's self-righteousness, Moses' reluctance to return to Egypt, or King David's abuse of power. Consistently, it is YHWH alone who accomplishes the deliverance.

Retelling the Story

Once known to all, Samson's incredible strength—especially when paired with his temper—made him fearsome to his enemies; nobody messed with Samson. Nobody. Then there were his drop dead good looks; in his day, everyone was taken with Samson's appearance. The muscles that gave him his strength and his thick, long black hair had much to do with why he was

For many years Manoah and his wife were childless. Manoah loved his wife very much but was very jealous of her. Evidence of his love was that he had neither divorced her nor taken another wife, though she had given birth to no child. When she told her husband that a tall, handsome angel had appeared to her and told her that she would bear a child, he was insane with jealousy. From this we can surmise that relationship problems ran in the family. (Josephus, *Antiquities*, V, 8.2-3)

Though Samson is described as so strong that he could pick up a mountain in each hand and clash them together like cymbals, he did have at least one physical imperfection, according to certain rabbis. Both his feet were deformed. But his personal imperfections were so great as to overshadow any physical limitation. He was swept away on a tide of passion when he saw beautiful women, especially beautiful Philistine women. At the same time the rabbis say he was unselfish in other ways, asking nothing for himself except strength to destroy the enemies of Israel. Perhaps the rabbis knew what we often try to overlook, that there has never been a hero without flaws. (Ginzberg IV, pp. 47-48)

listed annually in the tabloid *Israel's Sexiest Men*. And the ladies; suffice it to say, any woman he wanted could be his.

Proud, handsome Samson. Those who had known him and who remembered him could hardly believe what the Philistines had done to him. Most simply couldn't bear to look at him anymore.

The guilt and regret for what he had done took their toll. Giving away the secret of his strength to his paramour, the voluptuous and persistent Delilah, had cost him everything. When he fell, so did the spirits of his countrymen.

Now a fool in the courts of Philistine rulers, he was humiliated beyond belief. Blind and bald, Samson was, without question, *the* favorite entertainment at the great banquets thrown frequently for national leadership. For the attendees, Samson—stumbling around, beaten, jerked, prodded, and taunted mercilessly—was Israel, helpless and impotent in every sense. Samson could not forget what he heard time after time at these affairs.

"Hey, strong man, see if you can lift this heavy bowl for me. I can hardly move it."

"Over here, curly. Look at me when I talk to you! Listen, I want to ask you something kind of personal: Who's your barber?"

"Lover boy, what do you tell all those women who've been knocking at your door lately? 'Not tonight, honey. I have a headache you wouldn't believe'?"

"Whatcha lookin' at anyway? You know, I can't see your eyes from here, what color are they?"

The mocking laughter that filled the immense gatherings was the hardest part for this once-renowned warrior, but there was no let up. Furthermore, he was regarded as so harmless that he wasn't even tended by a prison guard; no, it was a Philistine child who led him from place to place. By now, Samson had no self-respect and little will to live.

After a time, Samson's hair began to grow back—ever so slowly—and no one really noticed. He realized that with the hair, some of his strength was returning as well. In time, it became clear to him what he had to do. Only one expression of personal dignity remained for him. In God's name and in the name of his people, he had to destroy the people who scorned him so.

One night, Samson knew the time was right. At a particularly large banquet, the Philistines put him on display between two giant pillars, where they could see him on their way to the roof. After a bit, he asked the boy who was his keeper to guide his hands to the pillars so that he could lean on them for a moment to get his breath. With the last ounce of strength he could muster, Samson pushed outward on both pillars. The roof came tumbling in, killing his enemies and him with them.

> Though his life was far from exemplary, Samson's death brought with it an unexpected blessing to Israel. The Philistines were so awestruck when Samson raged "against the dying of the light" (to borrow an apt phrase from Dylan Thomas) that they did not attack Israel for twenty years. (Ginzberg IV, p. 49)

Hannah

After her many years of praying and suffering ridicule, God grants Hannah a son, Samuel. But to gain her child, Hannah has promised to give him back to YHWH's service.

The Story

Her husband Elkanah said to her, 'Hannah, why are you crying and eating nothing? Why are you so miserable? Am I not more to you than ten sons?'

After they had finished eating and drinking at the sacrifice at Shiloh, Hannah rose in deep distress, and weeping bitterly stood before the LORD and prayed to him. Meanwhile Eli the priest was sitting on his seat beside the door of the temple of the LORD. Hannah made this vow: 'LORD of Hosts, if you will only take notice of my trouble and remember me, if you will not forget me but grant me offspring, then I shall give the child to the LORD for the whole of his life, and no razor shall ever touch his head.'

For a long time she went on praying before the LORD, while Eli watched her lips. Hannah was praying silently; her lips were moving although her voice could not be heard, and Eli took her for a drunken woman. 'Enough of this drunken behaviour!' he said to her. 'Leave off until the effect of the wine has gone.' 'Oh, sir!' she answered, 'I am a heart-broken woman; I have drunk neither wine nor strong drink, but I have been pouring out my feel-

ings before the LORD. Do not think me so devoid of shame, sir; all this time I have been speaking out of the depths of my grief and misery.' Eli said, 'Go in peace, and may the God of Israel grant what you have asked of him.' Hannah replied, 'May I be worthy of your kindness.' And no longer downcast she went away and had something to eat.

Next morning they were up early and, after prostrating themselves before the LORD, returned to their home at Ramah. Elkanah had intercourse with his wife Hannah, and the LORD remembered her; she conceived, and in due time bore a son, whom she named Samuel, 'because,' she said, 'I asked the LORD for him.'

Elkanah with his whole household went up to make the annual sacrifice to the LORD and to keep his vow. Hannah did not go; she said to her husband, 'After the child is weaned I shall come up with him to present him before the LORD; then he is to stay there always.' Her husband Elkanah said to her, 'Do what you think best; stay at home until you have weaned him. Only, may the LORD indeed see your vow fulfilled.' So the

50

woman stayed behind and nursed her son until she had weaned him.

When she had weaned him, she took him up with her. She took also a bull three years old, an ephah of flour, and a skin of wine, and she brought him, child as he was, into the house of the LORD at Shiloh. When the bull had been slaughtered, Hannah brought the boy to Eli and said, 'Sir, as sure as you live, I am the woman who stood here beside you praying to the LORD. It was this boy that I prayed for and the LORD has granted what I asked. Now I make him over to the LORD; for his whole life he is lent to the LORD.' And they prostrated themselves there before the LORD. . . .

Samuel continued in the service of the LORD, a mere boy with a linen ephod fastened round him. Every year his mother made him a little cloak and took it to him when she went up with her husband to offer the annual sacrifice. Eli would give his blessing to Elkanah and his wife and say, 'The LORD grant you children by this woman in place of the one whom you made over to the LORD.' Then they would return home.

Comments on the Story

An Israelite woman had to produce a baby. If she could not, she was regarded as less than a woman. This was a fact of life with which all Israelite women lived and a factor in a number of birth stories. Hannah's husband, Elkanah, had another wife, Peninnah, who was fertile, but Hannah could not bear children. Her husband said, "Am I not worth more to you than many children?" Perhaps these were generous words of comfort, but they also seem more to flatter Elkanah's own sense of importance than to give Hannah any assurance. Note that Hannah offers no answer to such a foolish question. Of course, no husband is worth one son, much less ten.

At this time there were many shrines in Israel, but the most important one was at Shiloh. Where the ancient Ark of the Covenant was kept, a hereditary priesthood conducted regular sessions of prayer and directed the offering of sacrificial animals to YHWH. The sacred shrine was located in a tent believed at the time to be the actual tent from which Moses and Aaron made offerings to YHWH in the wilderness.

Hannah went to the sacred site and prayed. Whether the fact of her praying or the method of her praying was unusual is not clear. In any case, as she prayed her lips moved but no sound came out. She prayed that if God would grant her a son she would give him back to YHWH. Eli, the priest, rebuked her for what he believed to be public drunkenness. He should talk! His sons, slated to succeed him as priests, had already developed a reputation for public drunkenness, embezzlement, and seduction of women on the Temple grounds.

But when Hannah explains that she is drunk on grief, not wine, since God had not seen fit to give her a son, Eli declares that YHWH will grant her petition. This gracious bestowal of Eli becomes a double-edged sword. YHWH

51

grants the son, but what Eli doesn't know is that in her grief Hannah has promised her son to the service of YHWH in the shrine. A year later she bears a son whom she names Samuel, and her response is a joyful song. It is widely believed that the "Song of Hannah" in fact is a much earlier piece of poetry, and that it was included here because of certain points of similarity between Hannah's emotional response and the flow of feeling in the poem. Many Christian interpreters have noticed the similarity of both the poem and the situation with the joyous song of Mary (Luke 1:46-55) in response to the announcement by the archangel that she would give birth to the Messiah.

Two points of contact between the poem and Hannah's situation stand out significantly. First, both include the theme of reversal—that YHWH will take those who have prominent positions in society and demote them to the bottom rung, while those poor and marginalized, the oppressed and mistreated, will rise in status. Certainly we are reminded of the elevation of Hannah's position, both in her own family and in Israelite society occasioned by the birth of her son.

There is a wonderful revolutionary notion contained in these verses. Many often assume that an exalted social or economic status is the direct result of God's blessings. There is a sublime confidence stated here that those who have the most will find themselves out in the cold at some future moment. The rich are not by nature of their wealth the blessed or chosen. God accomplishes the great reversal by raising up society's outcasts.

The second point of contact in the poem is the joyously ironic statement that the barren woman shall bear seven children, while the mother of children shall be forlorn, bereft of her offspring. One can almost hear the one-upmanship of Hannah against Peninnah, her rival in Elkanah's household.

Children born to once barren women in the Bible often find themselves in positions of prominence in Israel: Sarah, the mother of Isaac; Jacob and Esau from Rebekah; Joseph and Benjamin's mother, Rachel; Hannah, the mother of Samuel; Elizabeth in the New Testament, who gave birth to John the Baptist; and most prominently Mary, the mother of Jesus, not "barren" but certainly giving birth under the most abnormal of circumstances. Imbedded in these stories is the message that the weak, the powerless, receive preference from heaven, that sorrow and weeping will be replaced by joy and plenty, and that the comfortable and complacent will lose everything.

So this barren woman begins to sing when she receives a miracle baby, a gift from YHWH. When the child, Samuel, is weaned, she dutifully gives him back to God, leaving him in service to the high priest Eli at the sacred tent of Israel. Weaning occurred significantly later in Israel than in modern Western society, so Samuel might have been three or four years old when his mother left him at the sacred shrine.

Did Hannah's heart break at leaving her child? Did she feel proud? Once a year, on pilgrimage, she visited the boy and brought him a new set of clothes, his old set worn-out and outgrown. How hard it must have been to leave him each year. But with the resiliency of children, that was the life the boy Samuel knew and accepted. And having "lent" Samuel to YHWH, Hannah gives birth to five more children— not seven, as the poem says, but a respectable number just the same. People who are powerless, suffering the taunts and misuse of those with the strength and resources that they lack, can take encouragement from the story of Hannah.

Retelling the Story

Unlike so many of the young career women whom she knew, Ellen wanted children. All of her closer friends already had at least one child and were talking about having more. Those conversations were very difficult for Ellen. She was, by nature, a good listener and a supportive friend. But when the topic of children came up, she tried to change the subject; on more than one occasion, she had actually excused herself from a coffee or a meal so that her friends would not see her cry.

Ellen wanted children every bit as much as her friends did—probably more than most, she thought. She *desperately* wanted children, and she always had. Never once had she seen her demanding medical career as her primary calling. Though enormously successful as a physician, what she still wanted more than anything else was to be a mother.

Occasionally dealing in the clinics with those who abused their children, Ellen had an especially difficult time with the order of things in this world. Why did people who didn't even care about children often end up with more children than they could count? Why did God bless with children those women who neglected and otherwise mistreated their little ones? She simply could not understand.

Here she was with the ability to love children selflessly; she had the means to provide well for them in every way imaginable, but she had no children and no promise of any. "Why?" she would ask God. "Why!?" Why didn't *she* have the children instead of those who were ill-suited as mothers or who could take or leave children? At times, this really got to her. Her pain often became intense, and all she could do was to cry.

> Hannah's husband, Elkanah, was a just and compassionate man according to the rabbis. After ten years in a childless marriage he could have divorced his wife Hannah, but his love for her overcame even his desire for children. One day Hannah came to Elkanah and suggested that he take another wife, one who could bear children. It was only at his wife's insistence that Elkanah married Peninnah. In this fashion, say the rabbis, who ordinarily in later years disapproved of polygamy, this righteous man came to be married to two women. (Ginzberg VI, pp. 215-16)

53

The family of Elkanah was so pious that they went to the tent of meeting at Shiloh not only annually but three times during the year. And in every village and town the family passed through others were invited to join them. By this means more and more people were drawn back to the God of Israel, simply by this pious family's passing through their hometown. In order to multiply the faithful, the rabbis say, the family took a different route to Shiloh each time they went. (Ginzberg IV, pp. 57-58)

The rabbis say that God not only heard the frantic prayer of Hannah and answered it, but that it was God who planted the name Samuel in her heart as well. Since God heard Hannah's silent prayer, some among later generations allowed that certain prayers should be said silently instead of aloud. When it came time for Samuel to be born, some say, he was premature, born in the seventh month rather than the ninth. This is also said of Isaac and the prophets. (Ginzberg VI, p. 217)

Her husband, Philip, was very supportive of Ellen; he encouraged and comforted her and was always hopeful. But Ellen knew that he, too, wanted children as much as she did; her anxiety was increased because she also felt like a failure as his wife.

Needless to say, she had tried everything. She knew the best infertility doctors in the medical field; her own physicians had tried all treatments known to them, but she simply could not conceive. No one knew why.

She prayed without ceasing about her hurt and her wishes. A literate person theologically, she was surprised when she heard herself bargaining with God: "I'll do *anything,* anything at all if you will give me a child."

One morning, Ellen—who was never sick—awakened and was unmistakably nauseated. She went to work and made it through her morning rounds, and by lunch time, she felt better. But the next morning, the nausea was back. Could it be what she thought it would never be? Ellen called her obstetrician and said she had to see her that day. When she did see her doctor, the news was what she had been waiting all her life to hear. "Ellen, you're pregnant—six weeks or so."

"Thank you, Barbara. Thank you, God!" Ellen screamed. Her baby was on the way. This baby would share her lovely home, have the nicest clothes, go to the best schools, and—of course—be brought up in the church.

Eli's Sons and Samuel

The boy Samuel is awakened by a voice that neither he nor Eli recognizes at first. Then when they do understand that it is YHWH speaking, the words that God speaks through Samuel about Eli's sons are hard to take.

The Story

When Eli, now a very old man, heard a detailed account of how his sons were treating all the Israelites, and how they lay with the women who were serving at the entrance to the Tent of Meeting, he said to them, 'Why do you do such things? I hear from every quarter how wickedly you behave. Do stop it, my sons; for this is not a good report that I hear spreading among the Lord's people. If someone sins against another, God will intervene; but if someone sins against the Lord, who can intercede for him?' They would not listen, however, to their father's rebuke, for the Lord meant to bring about their death. The young Samuel, as he grew up, increasingly commended himself to the Lord and to the people. . . .

The boy Samuel was in the Lord's service under Eli. In those days the word of the Lord was rarely heard, and there was no outpouring of vision. One night Eli, whose eyes were dim and his sight failing, was lying down in his usual place, while Samuel slept in the temple of the Lord where the Ark of God was. Before the lamp of God had gone out, the Lord called him, and Samuel answered, 'Here I am!' and ran to Eli saying, 'You called me: here I am.' 'No, I did not call you,' said Eli; 'lie down again.' So he went and lay down. The Lord called Samuel again, and he got up and went to Eli. 'Here I am!' he said, 'Surely you called me.' 'I did not call, my son,' he answered; 'lie down again.' Samuel had not yet come to know the Lord, and the word of the Lord had not been disclosed to him. When the Lord called him for the third time, he again went to Eli and said, 'Here I am! You did call me.' Then Eli understood that it was the Lord calling the boy; he told Samuel to go and lie down and said, 'If someone calls once more, say, "Speak, Lord; your servant is listening." ' So Samuel went and lay down in his place.

Then the Lord came, and standing there called, 'Samuel, Samuel!' as before. Samuel answered, 'Speak, your servant is listening.' The Lord said, 'Soon I shall do something in Israel which will ring in the ears of all who hear it. When that day comes I shall make good every word from beginning to end that I have spoken against Eli and his family. You are to tell him that my judgement on his house will stand for ever because he knew of his sons' blasphemies against God and did not restrain them. Therefore I have sworn to the family of Eli that their abuse of sacrifices and offerings will never be expiated.'

Samuel lay down till morning, when he opened the doors of the house of the LORD; but he was afraid to tell Eli about the vision. Eli called Samuel: 'Samuel, my son!' he said; and Samuel answered 'Here I am!' Eli asked, 'What did the LORD say to you? Do not hide it from me. God's curse upon you if you conceal from me one word of all that he said to you.' Then Samuel told him everything, concealing nothing. Eli said, 'The LORD must do what is good in his eyes.'

As Samuel grew up, the LORD was with him, and none of his words went unfulfilled. From Dan to Beersheba, all Israel recognized that Samuel was attested as a prophet of the LORD. So the LORD continued to appear in Shiloh, because he had revealed himself there to Samuel. Samuel's word had authority throughout Israel.

Comments on the Story

Some theologians disagree about which is more important, the fact that God has spoken to someone or the content of what was said. For instance, many will argue that God's revelation to Job at the end of the book that bears his name is more important than what God tells Job. Some will even go so far as to argue that God's speech to Job is utter nonsense, and thus the content is not important. In this passage many interpreters have so marveled at the fact that God communicated with the boy Samuel that they lose sight of the content, which in this case makes for a far more interesting story.

Samuel, perhaps seven or eight years old, slept in the sacred tent, which served as the Israelite temple. It must have scared Samuel to sleep there, when Eli the high priest, and his family, slept in another tent nearby. How many times had he awakened in the night, terrified, with no mother to comfort him? Such details are left to the modern storyteller's imagination.

One night, Samuel heard a voice calling his name. He naturally assumed that Eli needed him for something. Samuel went to Eli and woke him, but the old man denied any knowledge of the voice.

As with many folktales, the action repeats three times. Eli, oblivious to so many things, takes three times to figure out what is going on. Although comic, the high priest's failure to discern the hand of YHWH is symptomatic of his fundamental spiritual blindness, which the narrator underscores when it becomes physical blindness later in life. The third time, Eli realizes that something is going on, and so he instructs Samuel the next time he hears the voice to respond with a formulaic expression of obedience: "Speak, for your servant is listening" (3:10).

Samuel does so, and he receives the first word from YHWH that anyone has heard for a long time. And most interpreters usually stop there—the boy who listened to the Lord. The story is so seductive, why go on?

But *what* YHWH says has far-reaching significance for Samuel's life as well as for the history of Israel. YHWH tells the young boy that his adopted father, the high priest, and his family are utterly corrupt and will be killed. For obvious reasons, Samuel fears sharing this news with Eli, but when pressed, he speaks bluntly. The old man meekly accepts the rebuke and spends the remainder of his life awaiting his fate. His sons die in battle a short time later, and Eli dies suddenly when he hears the news of their deaths.

But consider Samuel, whose first message from YHWH, is that God has rejected his adopted family. A vacuum remained that only Samuel could fill. The young boy could not have received it as good news. It was a burden and caused the breaking of hearts. Samuel, young and unformed, had lost two families before he reached his majority. This made him strong, but perhaps hard, too hard to understand and sympathize with the weakness of others.

And so that first communication set the tone for Samuel, and for most of prophecy in ancient Israel. It was a crushing burden, a burden that isolated Samuel and put him in opposition to most of society. And Samuel became king maker and king breaker, a fierce and giant figure in Israel.

This is an ambivalent episode in its tone. The form of the story is comic—the boy hearing voices, rushing to the old parent, only to be sent back to bed and to hear the voice again. The repetition of this activity gives almost a Keystone Cops structure to the narrative.

When Samuel finally responds to the voice and listens, the story takes a sudden turn toward the serious, even tragic. The boy must go to the priest, his surrogate father, and tell him the awful truth about his biological sons and their fate. It must take the same kind of courage for a member of an alcoholic or otherwise dysfunctional family to finally tell the truth about that family's situation.

This scene sets the tone for the rest of Samuel's life. He will have to face the people of Israel with the hazards of monarchy when they demand a king. And at YHWH's behest, he will choose a new king while the king Samuel anointed with his own hands still occupied the throne.

Retelling the Story

"The time has come for decision," evangelist Eldon Edwards said into the microphone, which perfectly enhanced his golden bass voice. "The time has come for decision. Right this very minute, you *must* decide whether you will walk with God toward heaven or with the devil toward hell."

Darrell Walker had heard Edwards's altar call hundreds of times. The people who had just listened to the already long and fiery sermon were getting ready to get up and sing the final hymn, but they were in for a big surprise. Edwards was on a roll and wouldn't give them the opportunity to sing for at least fifteen minutes more.

Darrell, for several years now, had been traveling around with Eldon Edwards and his sons, who provided the music for their father's revival meetings and evangelistic crusades. They were headquartered in Dalton, Georgia, which was Darrell's hometown. Actually, when Darrell was quite young, he had come to faith during one of their services there, and when he got old enough to go with them, his mother said it would be all right. He helped the Edwards family with setting up equipment, with controlling the sound during the singing and preaching, and with selling books by evangelist Eldon Edwards and cassette tapes of inspiring music by the Edwards Brothers, Slim and Jim, after the services.

At first, Darrell had been inspired by the time he spent with these men. They made a positive impact on many people's lives; they spoke and sang the gospel in the language understood by many rural folk no one else could have reached. Darrell still liked them all very much, but they weren't very inspiring to him anymore. Now, he helped out mainly for the spending money he made helping them.

> Some claim that the sins of Eli's sons were not so bad. They kept women who had come to offer a purification offering waiting so that they were delayed in returning to their families. But that was enough. (Ginzberg IV, p. 61)

Darrell would always remember how crushed he was the first time he had seen Eldon drunk out of his mind—and after a sermon, earlier that very night, on the evils of alcohol. "Letting even *one drop* pass your lips and get into your system is to violate the will of God and put yourself in danger of hell fire." (Eldon liked to mention hell frequently in his sermons.)

> Since Eli was not quick enough or stern enough in correcting his sons, he was punished, too. It is said that because of his sons' behavior he became old before his time. How many parents today could say the same! (Ginzberg IV, p. 61)

Darrell had gone to Edwards's room at the Lucky Strike Motel to make sure of the time he was supposed to be ready the next morning. "Brother Eldon," Darrell had screamed out at him, "you're drunk! You're drunk!"

"I wish you hadn't had to see this, boy," Eldon had said to him with tears suddenly in his eyes. "Brother Eldon has a sickness. Can you forgive him?"

And Slim and Jim slept with every woman they could find—most often women they met at their services. Darrell was constantly amazed that unmarried and married women of all ages, including those who praised the Lord most energetically during the singing and preaching, made themselves available for sexual favors. After initial contacts had been made, these women would keep in touch with the Edwards brothers, who certainly did more than sing. The best Darrell could tell, such sex was all either man lived for.

One night after a meeting in which twenty or thirty people had been saved, the four men were traveling back to their motel. Darrell was deeply troubled. "Something bothering you, boy?" Eldon asked him.

"Yes, sir," Darrell answered. "Can I talk with you when we get back?"

"Of course."

At the motel, Darrell went to Eldon Edwards's room. "What is it, boy?" Edwards asked him.

"Brother Eldon, I owe you so much. Please don't be hurt by what I have to say. Brother Eldon, the way you and your sons are living isn't right, and I'm afraid God is going to punish you, maybe even take your lives."

Phinehas was the better behaved of Eli's sons. But he was punished, too, because he did not attempt to correct his brother's ways. (Ginzberg IV, p. 61)

"Dear God, boy. Dear God."

Israel Wants a King

The people of Israel demanded a king, like other peoples, and after offering his objections Samuel reluctantly agrees.

The Story

So all the elders of Israel met, and came to Samuel at Ramah. They said to him, 'You are now old and your sons do not follow your ways; appoint us a king to rule us, like all the other nations.' But their request for a king displeased Samuel. He prayed to the LORD, and the LORD told them, 'Listen to the people and all that they are saying; they have not rejected you, it is I whom they have rejected, I whom they will not have to be their king. They are now doing to you just what they have done to me since I brought them up from Egypt: they have forsaken me and worshipped other gods. Hear what they have to say now, but give them a solemn warning and tell them what sort of king will rule them.'

Samuel reported to the people who were asking him for a king all that the LORD had said to him. 'This will be the sort of king who will bear rule over you,' he said. 'He will take your sons and make them serve in his chariots and with his cavalry, and they will run before his chariot. Some he will appoint officers over units of a thousand and units of fifty. Others will plough his fields and reap his harvest; others again will make weapons of war and equipment for the chariots. He will take your daughters for perfumers, cooks, and bakers. He will seize the best of your fields, vineyards, and olive groves, and give them to his courtiers. He will take a tenth of your grain and your vintage to give to his eunuchs and courtiers. Your slaves, both men and women, and the best of your cattle and your donkeys he will take for his own use. He will take a tenth of your flocks, and you yourselves will become his slaves. There will come a day when you will cry out against the king whom you have chosen; but the LORD will not answer you on that day.'

The people, however, refused to listen to Samuel. 'No,' they said, 'we must have a king over us; then we shall be like other nations, with a king to rule us, to lead us out to war and fight our battles.' When Samuel heard what the people had decided, he told the LORD, who said, 'Take them at their word and appoint them a king.' Samuel then dismissed all the Israelites to their homes.

Comments on the Story

Israel's relationship with the idea of monarchy shifted constantly. It was a point of major substantive debate on all levels and classes of Israelite society. We find that YHWH too appears ambiguous about the best system of government for this young nation. In Canaan, many of the native peoples were governed in small city-states, kings ruling over walled cities, surrounded by small agricultural villages that provided for the king and looked to him for protection. Israel up to this point was ruled tribally by elders, and in times of national emergency there would emerge a charismatic leader known as a judge.

There was strong hostility to the idea of a king. Many rejected monarchy at first, because for the Israelites to choose a king would constitute a rejection of YHWH. The second objection was that kings were commonly known to rule a hierarchical society in which the common people had few rights and labored to provide the king his opulent life-style.

Once before a man had declared himself a king, after the fashion of the Canaanite city-state rulers (see Judges 9). His brother stood on a raised area overlooking the city and called out a story about a group of plants and trees that wanted to make one of their number king.

They asked the olive tree, the fig tree, and the grape vine in turn to be their king. Each had more important things to do, producing fruit for the enjoyment of humanity.

Then they asked the thorn bush, which replied ominously, "Why, certainly I'll be your king." The implication here is that those who are not busy producing fruit have time to exert power over others.

Another time, earlier, a group of elders approached Gideon, a military hero, and asked him to establish a dynasty. He stated emphatically that only YHWH would be their king (see Judges 6–7). But there were always people who believed that Israel needed a more centralized, more stable government. Then the Israelites were defeated by the Philistines. They lost badly—the Philistines destroyed not only Israel's army, but also its central place of worship and most of its leadership, and most painful of all to the Israelites, the Philistines captured the Ark as a trophy, which they presented to their god, Dagon. Throughout, however, Samuel managed to hold the country together.

But when Samuel grew old and prepared to appoint his incompetent and dishonest sons to govern after him, the elders demanded that Samuel appoint a king. The people, having been decisively defeated and subjugated by the Philistines, now feared that they would once again be left without an effective leader.

Samuel responded angrily, but why did the news upset him so? The narrative informs us that it is YHWH who is angry at Israel's rejection of him, and Samuel cannot tolerate such unfaithfulness.

Were they not rejecting Samuel and his leadership, too? YHWH's argument highlights Samuel's hurt feelings: "They have not rejected you [Samuel], but they have rejected me [YHWH] from being king over them" (Judg. 8:7). YHWH would not need to say as much unless Samuel felt rejected in the first place—which is not to mention the unspoken rejection of Samuel's worthless sons. Couldn't there perhaps be some self-interest in Samuel's displeasure at the people's request for a king? The line between what YHWH wants and what God's spokespersons desire is always a difficult one to distinguish. This ambiguity is always present when we look for God's hand and God's will to be active in the world.

Samuel reports that the tribal elders had hurt YHWH with their request, and that a king is the worst thing they could want. He gives them a list of all the terrible things a king will do (a list astonishingly similar to the excesses of Solomon, Israel's third king). A king would take their children to be his soldiers and servants. Their field work would not feed them but would serve the king's table. He would appropriate the best land, orchards, and vineyards for himself. In effect, a king would make slaves of all his people. However, they refuse to be dissuaded, rejecting YHWH's and Samuel's political advice.

So Samuel tells the people that YHWH will grudgingly grant their demand, and they leave satisfied. Of course, after a false start (the first king, Saul), the Israelites choose a king, David, of whom YHWH would say, "Your throne shall be established forever" (2 Sam. 7:16).

YHWH's final endorsement of the monarchy leaves us confused. Is monarchy a rejection of YHWH or YHWH's highest will? Either YHWH has changed the divine mind, or the political and religious pronouncements of certain people in power about YHWH's intentions are deeply motivated by self-interest. Whatever kind of government we might want, we often assume to be God's will.

Is God giving in to human weakness, teaching these people a lesson? Perhaps the fear of the monarchy is linked with the fear of idolatry, that the king will be honored in place of YHWH. Is that why we find such terrible, truthful stories about the lives of Israel's kings? Maybe through these frighteningly honest stories we will finally realize that "There is no other God but YHWH" and that the king "puts his pants on one leg at a time, just as we do"—and gets caught with them down sometimes.

Retelling the Story

"Samuel, you mustn't take this personally. We have nothing against you, absolutely nothing. The point simply is this: We must have a strong, godly leader. If your sons had followed in your footsteps, if they shared even some of your values, then everything would be different, but we will not survive as a nation with any of your sons leading us. Can you not understand our needs and our fears? Samuel, please!" The pleadings of the Israelite people went on and on, but old Samuel vacillated between not understanding them and being infuriated at their demands.

"You don't know what you're saying. You don't know what you need. Only God knows what you need, and God has always provided the leaders of our people. To try and interfere, to be audacious enough to try and tell God what to do, will bring God's judgments upon all of us." Samuel was adamant in his refusal to honor the wishes of the people to whom he had taught the ways of God for most of his life. Had they not understood any of what he had told them about God?

The people persisted, however, and finally—in frustration—Samuel went to God with the request of the people. Samuel told God that the people of Israel now wanted a king like all the other nations. And God's response surprised Samuel.

"If they want a king," God said, "then that is what they will get."

"Excuse me, God," Samuel stuttered, "my hearing isn't what it used to be. I thought I heard you say that if the people want a king, then you will see that they get a king."

"That's right, Samuel. Tell them what I said, but you must also tell them that there will be a price to pay for

> The desire for a king was not necessarily offensive to God. Considering how some of the judges behaved, it was little surprise that the people would want to replace their judges with a king. The thing that angered God was the way the people phrased their request and the reason they gave for wanting a king. "Give us a king," they said *"so we can be like the other nations."* (Ginzberg IV, p. 64)

> There was real disagreement on God's role in establishing the monarchy in Israel. Some of the rabbis say that God intended that Israel have a king, the only objection being the language in which the request was phrased. Others say that timing was the problem. The people shouldn't have asked for a king until *after* they had built the Temple. Still others propose that God did not think that a monarchy was best for Israel but allowed it, giving the people the opportunity to live with the consequences of their choice. (Ginzberg VI, p. 230)

monarchical rule. Their king isn't going to work and rule for free. He will fill his coffers full by taking a tenth of all my people have and by putting their daughters and sons to work for him. It will be a harder life than they have known before, but this is what they will have. This is my judgment upon them," explained God, "and either they will suffer because of it or they will find a way to make it work to my glory and to their good. Tell them all that I have said, Samuel."

Apparently Samuel was of the opinion that God allowed, but didn't necessarily approve of, the establishment of a monarchy in Israel. The rabbis differ on why the prophet tells the people all the terrible things a king will do to them and their children. Some say that all the powers he describes are truly given to the king. Others say he was simply telling the people the most frightening tactics of an evil king. (Ginzberg VI, pp. 230-31)

So Samuel went to the leaders among his people and told them what God had made known to him. He warned them once again of the dangers of changing the way they had been ruled in the past and of the mechanics of how a king paid the expenses of a kingdom. Samuel thought surely they would not want a king when they understood what was involved, but they did. They continued to insist on a king to rule them.

After that, God told Samuel to follow the divine lead and get to the business of appointing a king for the people of Israel. And the bewildered old prophet, Samuel, set out to do the bidding of God.

Samuel Chooses David

While Saul still reigns on the throne of Israel, Samuel goes to Bethle-hem and chooses from among Jesse's sons another king, David.

The Story

The LORD said to Samuel, 'How long will you grieve because I have rejected Saul as king of Israel? Fill your horn with oil and take it with you; I am sending you to Jesse of Bethle-hem; for I have chosen myself a king from among his sons.' Samuel answered, 'How can I go? If Saul hears of it, he will kill me.' 'Take a heifer with you,' said the LORD; 'say you have come to offer a sacrifice to the LORD, and invite Jesse to the sac-rifice; then I shall show you what you must do. You are to anoint for me the man whom I indicate to you.' Samuel did as the LORD had told him, and went to Bethlehem, where the elders came in haste to meet him, saying, 'Why have you come? Is all well?' 'All is well,' said Samuel; 'I have come to sacrifice to the LORD. Purify yourselves and come with me to the sacrifice.' He himself purified Jesse and his sons and invited them to the sacrifice.

When they came, and Samuel saw Eliab, he thought, 'Surely here, before the LORD is his anointed king.' But the LORD said to him, 'Pay no attention to his outward appearance and stature, for I have rejected him. The LORD does not see as a mortal sees; mortals see only appearances but the LORD sees into the heart.' Then Jesse called Abinadab and had him pass before Samuel, but he said, 'No, the LORD has not chosen this one.' Next he presented Shammah, of whom Samuel said, 'Nor has the LORD chosen him.' Seven of his sons were presented to Samuel by Jesse, but he said, 'The LORD has not chosen any of these.'

Samuel asked, 'Are these all the sons you have?' 'There is still the youngest,' replied Jesse, 'but he is looking after the sheep.' Samuel said to Jesse, 'Send and fetch him; we will not sit down until he comes.' So he sent and fetched him. He was handsome, with ruddy cheeks and bright eyes. The LORD said, 'Rise and anoint him: this is the man.' Samuel took the horn of oil and anointed him in the presence of his brothers, and the spirit of the LORD came upon David and was with him from that day onwards. Then Samuel set out on his way to Ramah.

Comments on the Story

Samuel was locked in a terrible power struggle with Saul, the king. Samuel, the old patriarchal figure, leaves the king dumbfounded by pronouncing his political and personal doom in strong language and no uncertain terms: "Now your kingdom will not continue; [YHWH] has sought out a man after his own heart" (1 Sam. 13:14). "[YHWH] has rejected you from being king over Israel. . . . [YHWH] has torn the kingdom of Israel from you this very day" (1 Sam. 15:26, 28).

Later, Samuel goes to seek another Israelite family and YHWH tells him to choose the new leader from among the sons. David is the youngest. All his older brothers, more likely choices, are rejected by YHWH. What was David like when he was chosen by this strange man? The text describes him as "ruddy, with beautiful eyes" (1 Sam. 16:12), which in this context may mean either beautiful or, more likely, unformed, young, not yet qualified to do business with the elders of the tribe. (See 1 Sam. 17:42, where the Philistines use the term disparagingly concerning David.)

Further, David is least impressive in the procession of sons. The structure of the story here is exactly that of the Cinderella story—instead of stepsisters, David's older brothers do not consider him important enough to appear before Samuel. David kept the sheep, probably a lower status job in the family, which underscores his inferior status with his brothers. While they deal with important matters, he is stuck in the meadows. (Later, they mock him before his battle with Goliath.)

And instead of a glass slipper, Samuel's prophetic insight separates the one truly called by YHWH. Each brother is rejected in turn, although each initially appears suitable to Samuel's spiritually limited vision. YHWH corrects Samuel: "Do not look on his appearance or on the height of his stature, because I have rejected him; for [YHWH] does not see as mortals see; they look on the outward appearance, but [YHWH] looks on the heart" (1 Sam. 16:7). This pronouncement appears rather odd coming from a God who first chose handsome Saul to be king. Some years earlier, Samuel burst with pride when he bragged about how good looking Saul was: "When he took his stand among the people, he was head and shoulders taller than any of them. Samuel said to all the people, 'Do you see the one whom [YHWH] has chosen? There is no one like him among all the people'" (1 Sam. 10:23-24). How different our world would be if people tried to look beyond the appearance of people and saw something of their inward character. Even today we strive so diligently to conform to some outward image and neglect to develop our inner selves. It is indeed comforting to know that God does not seem to care about outer images at all. What does this story have to say about our current value system?

What an odd episode this is! A boy, perhaps as young as twelve, is told by YHWH's prophet of such transformation, advancement, power. How does a child live with such knowledge? Did David take it seriously? Was David very moved? At this very moment, did the wheels in his mind begin turning? Even at this young age, did he begin to calculate means to achieve the end—how he could become the king of Israel? In subsequent stories we will see that David's calculating ambition grew to be virtually limitless.

Retelling the Story

Saul didn't work out, not at all. For one thing, he wasn't, shall we say, well balanced. For another, when given the opportunity to do so, he had not put God first, and the nation of Israel was in bad shape. God said that it was time for a change, and it was as if Saul had never been king. God bypassed him altogether; Saul had no say whatsoever in leaving his throne or in naming his successor. Saul sat passively and helplessly by while the events of his undoing took place before his eyes.

God brought old Samuel out of retirement to tap another king—Samuel complaining all the while. "No disrespect, God, but I've served my time. What's more, if you don't mind my saying so, my record in choosing kings for you isn't exactly encouraging. Look at the job Saul has done; he's not a bad guy, really, but he has turned out to be a rotten king. And if he hears that I'm out on a recruiting trip for a new king, he will kill me. He will have no patience with me; Saul will be furious with me even if I tell him that I am simply doing your will. He will have me killed."

"Samuel, you are the one who must serve me in this way. Now get on with it. I have already chosen Israel's next king, and I promise you that it's going to work this time. All you need to do is to pack up your things for the trip, fill your horn with oil for the anointing, and go to the house of Jesse the Bethlehemite."

"Retirement's not so bad; I'd really rather not have things end right now. I'm sure you understand. God, why don't you get a younger man to anoint the next king? Maybe he will better hear you. Maybe he will do an improved job of finding the man whom your people need as their leader."

"Samuel," God said, "this is the only way you can redeem yourself. Now go!"

The rabbis pay a great deal of attention to David's ancestry. Some say that Miriam, sister to Aaron and Moses, was his forebear. His great-grandmother was Ruth, Naomi's faithful daughter-in-law. His grandfather, Obed, was a true servant of God, as his name implies (*Obed* means "servant"). David's father, Jesse, is portrayed by some as being a great scholar. Jesse was also such a good man that if God had not decided that all human beings would die after the first pair exited the Garden of Eden, Jesse would have lived forever. (Ginzberg IV, p. 81)

David is said to have had a ruddy complexion, though in some cases the same verses have been interpreted to mean that he had red hair. Some say that this was a result of the heat of Jesse's passion when his son was conceived. Others say it was simply a sign (one that Samuel recognized) that he would shed much blood during his life. Noticing how different from them the boy David looked, his brothers suspected that he was not their father's son and wanted to kill him and their mother. Jesse put a stop to their plan but compromised by treating David as if he were a slave. The boy was sent away to tend Jesse's sheep for twenty-eight years. (Ginzberg IV, p. 247; *Antiquities* VI, 8.1)

Even the oil in the anointing horn reacted to David's presence. When Samuel attempted to anoint David's brothers the oil would not budge from the horn. But when David came near, the horn emptied horn emptied its contents all by itself, and the oil ran down the young shepherd's head and shoulders. Some even say that the drops landing on his clothes turned into pearls and precious stones. (Ginzberg IV, p. 84)

Old bones creaking and strength long since waned, Samuel loaded up his pack mule and with his assistant headed to Bethlehem. Once there, Samuel went straight to Jesse's home and told him that he needed to see his sons. One by one, they came and stood before Samuel. The first son, Eliab, had *king* written all over his face. Samuel was ready to break out the anointing oil and have this job done, but God said, "No, Samuel. Keep looking." So the other sons came, but Samuel didn't get the signals from God that either would be the next king of Israel.

Frustrated, Samuel said to Jesse, "Is this all? I've seen all your sons?"

"For practical purposes, yes sir, you have."

"I don't get it," Samuel complained. "Something's wrong somewhere. I knew I should be here."

"Sir," Jesse said to Samuel, "I do have one other son, my youngest, who is out in the field tending the sheep, but he is too young to take on any major responsibility. He's just a boy."

"Let me see him," Samuel insisted.

David came and stood before the old prophet who, in spite of himself, still had the vision to see the hand of God at work.

David and the Philistine Giant

*David, still a boy, kills the giant Goliath after all the soldiers of Saul
are afraid to face the massive Philistine.*

The Story

The Philistines mustered their
forces for war; they massed at
Socoh in Judah and encamped
between Socoh and Azekah at Ephes-
dammim. Saul and the Israelites also
mustered, and they encamped in the
valley of Elah. They drew up their
lines of battle facing the Philistines,
the Philistines occupying a position
on one hill and the Israelites on
another, with a valley between them.

A champion came out from the
Philistine camp, a man named
Goliath, from Gath; he was over nine
feet in height. He had a bronze helmet on his head, and he wore plate
armour of bronze, weighing five thousand shekels. On his legs were bronze
greaves, and one of his weapons was a
bronze dagger. The shaft of his spear
was like a weaver's beam, and its
head, which was of iron, weighed six
hundred shekels. His shield-bearer
marched ahead of him.

The champion stood and shouted
to the ranks of Israel, 'Why do you
come out to do battle? I am the Philistine champion and you are Saul's
men. Choose your man to meet me. If
he defeats and kills me in fair fight,
we shall become your slaves; but if I
vanquish and kill him, you will be our

slaves and serve us. Here and now I
challenge the ranks of Israel. Get me
a man, and we will fight it out.' When
Saul and the Israelites heard what the
Philistine said, they were all shaken
and deeply afraid.

David was the son of an Ephrathite
called Jesse, who had eight sons, and
who by Saul's time had become old,
well advanced in years. His three
eldest sons had followed Saul to the
war; the eldest was called Eliab, the
next Abinadab, and the third
Shammah; David was the youngest.
When the three eldest followed Saul,
David used to go from attending Saul
to minding his father's flocks at Bethlehem.

Morning and evening for forty days
the Philistine came forward and took
up his stance. Then one day Jesse
said to his son David, 'Take your
brothers an ephah of this roasted
grain and these ten loaves of bread,
and go with them as quickly as you
can to the camp. These ten cream-
cheeses are for you to take to their
commanding officer. See if your
brothers are well and bring back some
token from them.' Saul and the brothers and all the Israelites were in the
valley of Elah, fighting the Philistines.

Early next morning David, having left someone in charge of the sheep, set out on his errand and went as Jesse had told him. He reached the lines just as the army was going out to take up position and was raising the war cry. The Israelites and the Philistines drew up their ranks opposite each other. David left his things in the charge of the quartermaster, ran to the line, and went up to his brothers to greet them. While he was talking with them the Philistine champion, Goliath from Gath, came out from the Philistine ranks and issued his challenge in the same words as before; and David heard him. When the Israelites saw the man they fell back before him in fear.

'Look at this man who comes out day after day to defy Israel,' they said. 'The king is to give a rich reward to the man who kills him; he will also give him his daughter in marriage and will exempt his family from service due in Israel.' David asked the men near him, 'What is to be done for the man who kills this Philistine and wipes out this disgrace? And who is he, an uncircumcised Philistine, to defy the armies of the living God?' The soldiers, repeating what had been said, told him what was to be done for the man who killed him.

David's elder brother Eliab overheard him talking with the men and angrily demanded, 'What are you doing here? And whom have you left to look after those few sheep in the wilderness? I know you, you impudent young rascal; you have only come to see the fighting.' David answered, 'Now what have I done? I only asked a question.' He turned away from him to someone else and repeated his question, but everybody gave him the same answer.

David's words were overheard and reported to Saul, who sent for him. David said to him, 'Let no one lose heart! I shall go and fight this Philistine.' Saul answered, 'You are not able to fight this Philistine; you are only a lad, and he has been a fighting man all his life.' David said to Saul, 'Sir, I am my father's shepherd; whenever a lion or bear comes and carries off a sheep from the flock, I go out after it and attack it and rescue the victim from its jaws. Then if it turns on me, I seize it by the beard and batter it to death. I have killed lions and bears, and this uncircumcised Philistine will fare no better than they; he has defied the ranks of the living God. The LORD who saved me from the lion and the bear will save me from this Philistine,' 'Go then,' said Saul; 'and the LORD be with you.'

He put his own tunic on David, placed a bronze helmet on his head, and gave him a coat of mail to wear; he then fastened his sword on David over his tunic. But David held back, because he had not tried them, and said to Saul, 'I cannot go with these, because I am not used to them.' David took them off, then picked up his stick, chose five smooth stones from the wadi, and put them in a shepherd's bag which served as his pouch, and, sling in hand, went to meet the Philistine.

The Philistine, preceded by his shield-bearer, came on towards David. He looked David up and down and had nothing but disdain for this lad with his ruddy cheeks and bright eyes. He said to David, 'Am I a dog that you come out against me with sticks?' He cursed him in the name of his god, and said, 'Come, I shall give your flesh to the birds and the beasts.'

David answered, 'You have come against me with sword and spear and dagger, but I come against you in the name of the LORD of Hosts, the God of the ranks of Israel which you have defied. The LORD will put you into my power this day; I shall strike you down and cut your head off and leave your carcass and the carcasses of the Philistines to the birds and the wild beasts; the whole world will know that there is a God in Israel. All those who are gathered here will see that the LORD saves without sword or spear; the battle is the LORD's, and he will put you all into our power.'

Comments on the Story

Once I taught this passage in a religion class for junior high boys. I was equipped with what I considered a fine interpretation: David represented the believer; Goliath stood for the giant problems that junior high boys face.

I began to make the connections as to how by faith we defeat life's adversities, but they interrupted me and finished the whole lesson in unison by parroting exactly my facile moralizing.

Why do we feel moved to allegorize this story by turning it into something like an episode from Bunyan's *Pilgrim's Progress?* Like these young boys we have probably heard such an interpretation numerous times in various settings, but even now we strain to see beyond it.

It is rather odd that a realistic narrative would contain such fantastical figures as giants, from Israel's mythic history. Giants had become in the Israelite sensibility a throwback to the legendary past when magic existed much closer to the surface of life and the gods could be more readily and frequently encountered. Giants were the embodiment of evil, malevolent forces in Israelite stories. They existed in primeval times when things were different and gods walked the earth. They shared of the substance of both gods and humans, as in Genesis 6 when the gods' children joined with human women and produced giants. In most of the ancient stories, one had to overcome giants in order to pass from childhood to adulthood, as David had to. This very fact may account for the ease with which this story applies to the struggles of the young for maturity.

So David defeated the powers of chaos, that evil force seeking to overcome good, when he overcame the Philistine giant. It is no wonder that when the Israelite army marched victoriously back from the battle, the women sang:

> Saul has killed his thousands,
> But David his tens of thousands.
> (1 Sam. 18:7)

Many scholars believe that very early on, the Israelite kings, in imitation of grander Babylonian practices, reenacted the battle between the gods of chaos and those of order and society. The king would ceremoniously drive out the evil gods of chaos. This ritual act in Babylon (and perhaps Israel) ensured the continued existence of the orderly universe. This might provide one reason for the popularity of the Goliath story.

And so David delivered Israel from its hated enemies. Perhaps, if we delve more deeply than the pious allegories of nineteenth- and twentieth-century popular Christian psychology, we would see this as more than an allegory of the individual believer's struggle. Instead, we might better see the significance of this narrative in a wider context in which this legendary figure, the future King David, is rescuing the land from the chaotic forces.

One way to interpret this narrative is as an adventure story, exciting and suspenseful. The underdog defeats the arrogant and (seemingly) superior opponent using wit and stealth to overcome strength and mass. We are wrong to think that every exciting story must have a clearly stated point, theological or philosophical. To leave people breathless is reason enough to tell this tale.

The horror of the chaotic giant only serves to increase the suspense—this underdog faces a hostile universe that even the bravest of soldiers fear. The victory is thereby so much sweeter, for David and for us. To enable people to experience both the excitement of building suspense and that sweetness and relief is an accomplishment the best of storytellers hope for.

Even as a youngster David brought order to Israel and became wildly popular. And as with the lives of many dictators, we are compelled to question the trade off—what is lost when people invest so much power into a single individual, and surrender so much freedom, so that law and order might be assured.

Retelling the Story

Just as David was reputed to be a descendant of Ruth, some rabbis suggest that Goliath came from the line of Orpah. In the story in Ruth the two Moabite women were sisters-in-law, but some sages suggest that they were sisters as well. Both were said to be daughters of Eglon, the king of Moab. (Ginzberg IV, p. 85).

My four-year-old son, Jonathan, often asks to hear the story of David and Goliath. "Tell me about the great Goliath Gath!" he says. It always strikes me that he does not ask for the story of the small lad David. He looks at his big brother and laments, "Am I going to be David because I am the littlest?" and so we hear again about the plate of armor and bronze and the bronze greaves. We talked for some time one afternoon about the bronze greaves. Now Jonathan wants greaves cut from brown paper bags and held on with rubber bands. He looks down at them and grins his approval. And then there is the spear to talk about, the spear like a weaver's beam and its heavy iron head. Jonathan walks around the kitchen roaring his strength.

"And what did David take to his brothers in battle?" I ask. Jonathan smiles because he knows this ritual well. I start him off by saying, "He brought ten loaves of bread and . . ." Jonathan quickly jumps in, for this is his part, "And ten cheeses." He says these words with great satisfaction. I look at him and wonder what pleases him so much.

Then I must repeat the part about David's taking of Saul's armor. "Why?" he asks, "Why did he take it off? He did not even have a sword, and Goliath was so big." But he did have five smooth stones. "Like the ones from the lake?" Jonathan wants to

> Some traditions say that David's father, Jesse, thought the boy was slow to learn and consequently put him to tending sheep. Others say that David's looks were so plain that when Samuel came to Jesse's house, the prophet didn't even notice the youngster. It was God who spoke to Samuel, saying, "Why are you sitting down when the one I have chosen is standing?" Only then did Samuel recognize the next king of Israel. (Ginzberg VI, p. 249)

know. Yes, and we find the oval gray rocks, smooth and lined with black and brown. He holds the rocks quietly, and I see him measuring their weight against bronze plate armor.

As Jonathan grows he will come to know the land of the valley of Elah. He will often walk the hills and valleys between his Goliath and David. There will be days when he will feel large and loud. He will be long striding and full of appetite. There will be times when he will need to be unassailable, even unapproachable. His armor will need to be bright bronze and his command will need to be unwavering. Yet this Goliath part of himself will not bind up every other character within him, for then he would be only hairy and blustering, roaring in the blazing sun out over the valleys to no one.

There will also be a figure out of the back hills of himself, a young laughing figure who will be clever and small. He will come with his bread and cheeses and be unwelcome. There will be the serious work of daily battle to accomplish, and this young one will appear to be useless, interfering, impudent. He will rearrange the expectations of the day. He will refuse armor and will refuse to roar beneath the sun. He will enter a dwelling, recline on pillows, and play the harp. Impudent or not, he will ask his questions and turn away from the doubts and uncertainties. He will trust the things he has tried and found to be true, and they will be simple. His knowledge is deeper than first thought. He has been frightened and has endured. He has been attacked and has been able to rescue himself. On those brown-green hills and among those valleys, the two figures will collide within my son as they collide within us all.

I remember when we all visited Grandma. She had been suffering from Alzheimer's for several years, and though she recognized us, she could not

As soon as David looked the Philistine giant in the eye, Goliath could not move. This rattled the soldier so that he started making foolish threats. For example, he said, "Come any closer and I'll feed you to the cattle." That was a stupid thing to say, since everyone knows that cattle don't eat meat. So David shouted back, "The birds will peck your bones clean." After the young man said that, Goliath tilted his head back to look up for the birds. This was just enough for the young shepherd to place a stone from his sling right in the gap between the giant's visor and his helmet. (Ginzberg IV, p. 87).

speak coherently except for sudden, brief sentences. Her thin hands shook as she slowly managed to remove crumbs from the corner of her mouth. And then her hand would travel hesitantly to the side of her soft wrinkled face, where she would try to pat a few gray hairs into place. Jonathan stood very still and watched her.

I bustled around the room, arranging cards and flowers. "How pretty you look today, Mom," I said in a loud voice. "And look at the blue sky. Did you ever see such a blue? There are only a few clouds, and they are all white. No chance of rain today. Oh, but are you chilly? Here's a sweater. Lean forward. That's great. You did well, Mom. Here's your catch ball. Let's play catch. Here we go! Oh, good catch, Mom. Now let go. Let go of the ball. Thank you, Mom. Here's a little chocolate. Would you like a little chocolate, Mom? Open your mouth. Open your mouth, Mom. It's chocolate. Don't you want a little chocolate? Come on, Mom. That's good. Do you like the chocolate, Mom?"

I suddenly saw Jonathan walking over to where his grandmother was sitting. He took her hand in his and patted it softly and did not let it go. Then he turned to me and said, "Grandma isn't talking, Mommy, because she's just a little shy." And without another word, he put his arm around her neck, leaned over, and kissed her cheek. I went to them and embraced them both. As I moved away, my mother's eyes met mine. Slowly she whispered, "He knows." Her eyes brightened and closed, and her lips gently parted as she smiled.

Michal and David

*David marries Michal, Saul's daughter, then leaves, fearing his life at
her father's hand. When the Ark is returned, David dances and Michal
ridicules him.*

The Story

Saul said to David, 'Here is my elder daughter Merab; I shall give her to you in marriage, but in return you must serve me valiantly and fight the LORD's battles.' For Saul meant David to meet his end not at his hands but at the hands of the Philistines. David answered Saul, 'Who am I and what are my father's people, my kinsfolk, in Israel, that I should become the king's son-in-law?' However, when the time came for Saul's daughter Merab to be married to David, she had already been given to Adriel of Meholah.

But Michal, Saul's other daughter, fell in love with David, and when Saul was told of this, he saw that it suited his plans. He said to himself, 'I will give her to him; let her be the bait that lures him to his death at the hands of the Philistines.' So Saul proposed a second time to make David his son-in-law, and ordered his courtiers to say to David privately, 'The king is well disposed to you and you are dear to us all; now is the time for you to marry into the king's family.' When they spoke in this way to David, he said to them, 'Do you think that marrying the king's daughter is a matter of so little consequence that a poor man of no account, like myself, can do it?'

The courtiers reported what David had said, and Saul replied, 'Tell David this: all the king wants as the bride-price is the foreskins of a hundred Philistines, by way of vengeance on his enemies.' Saul was counting on David's death at the hands of the Philistines. The courtiers told David what Saul had said, and marriage with the king's daughter on these terms pleased him well. Before the appointed time, David went out with his men and slew two hundred Philistines; he brought their foreskins and counted them out to the king in order to be accepted as his son-in-law. Saul then married his daughter Michal to David. He saw clearly that the LORD was with David, and knew that Michal his daughter had fallen in love with him; and he grew more and more afraid of David and was his enemy for the rest of his life. . . .

Saul sent servants to keep watch on David's house, intending to kill him in the morning. But David's wife Michal warned him to get away that night, 'or tomorrow,' she said, 'you will be a dead man.' She let David down through a window and he slipped away and escaped. Michal then took their household god and put it on the bed; at its head she laid a goat's-hair rug and covered it all with a cloak. When the men arrived to arrest David she told them he was ill. Saul, however, sent them back to see David for themselves, 'Bring him to me, bed and all,' he ordered, 'so that I may kill him.' When they came, there was the household god on the bed and the goat's-hair rug at its head. Saul said to Michal, 'Why have you played this trick on me and let my enemy get away?' Michal answered, 'He said to me, "Help me to escape or I shall kill you." ' . . .

Saul meanwhile had given his daughter Michal, David's wife, to Palti son of Laish from Gallim. . . .

Abner sent envoys on his own behalf to David with the message, 'Who is to control the land? Let us come to terms, and you will have my support in bringing the whole of Israel over to you.' David's answer was: 'Good, I will come to terms with you, but on one condition: that you do not come into my presence without bringing Saul's daughter Michal to me.' David also sent messengers to Saul's son Ishbosheth with the demand: 'Hand over to me my wife Michal for whom I gave a hundred Philistine foreskins as the bride-price.' Thereupon Ishbosheth sent and took her from her husband Paltiel son of Laish. Her husband followed her as far as Bahurim, weeping all the way, until Abner ordered him back, and he went. . . .

. . . As the Ark of the LORD was entering the City of David, Saul's daughter Michal looked down from a window and saw King David leaping and whirling before the LORD, and she despised him in her heart.

After they had brought the Ark of the LORD, they put it in its place inside the tent that David had set up for it, and David offered whole-offerings and shared-offerings before the LORD. Having completed these sacrifices, David blessed the people in the name of the LORD of Hosts, and distributed food to them all, a flat loaf of bread, a portion of meat, and a cake of raisins, to every man and woman in the whole gathering of the Israelites. Then all the people went home.

David returned to greet his household, and Michal, Saul's daughter, came out to meet him. She said, 'What a glorious day for the king of Israel, when he made an exhibition of himself in the sight of his servants' slave-girls, as any vulgar clown might do!' David answered her, 'But it was done in the presence of the LORD, who chose me instead of your father and his family and appointed me prince over Israel, the people of the LORD. Before the LORD I shall dance for joy, yes, and I shall earn yet more disgrace and demean myself still more in your eyes; but those slave-girls of whom you speak; they will hold me in honour for it.'

To her dying day Michal, Saul's daughter, was childless.

Comments on the Story

This sad love story appeared doomed from the outset. Michal, the king's daughter, fell in love with the good-looking, charismatic newcomer, David. David was a Bethlehemite at the royal court, a country boy living in the fast lane, who was rising to increasing influence and prominence in the Israelite bureaucracy. Michal had a schoolgirl crush on this popular older boy.

When Saul (her father, the king) heard about her feelings, it suited his political purposes to arrange his daughter's betrothal to David. Previously he tried to arrange David's marriage to Michal's older sister, but David had refused. Saul, we are told, wanted David to marry so that he might demand an impossible bride price that David's pride would compel him to accept and would be killed in the process.

David's reasons for entering into this relationship are not clear, but the narrator tells us not that David loved Michal, but rather that it pleased him to become the king's son-in-law. Michal expressed her attachment to David in terms of her emotions; David covered his response in terms of political advancement.

Saul demanded one hundred Philistine foreskins, which would obviously require killing at least one hundred Philistines, for it is not likely that Philistine soldiers would lie still for such a surgical operation while alive. David took his men and killed two hundred Philistines and deposited the pile of foreskins before the king in his throne room.

Saul is held to his bargain as David and Michal are married. Saul's jealousy and suspicion of David increase until the young bridegroom must run away to preserve his life. Michal risks her own life to protect David, concealing his escape by placing a David-sized sculpted figure in her husband's bed. Saul's soldiers do not discover that David has slipped out until the next day.

At this point in the story, David drops Michal utterly. While remaining a fugitive in the southern part of Israel, his own tribal territory, he marries twice and makes no effort to rejoin Michal, or even send her word as to his whereabouts.

Michal declares herself divorced, and Saul, her father, finds her a new husband from the ruling families of Gibeah, the capital. She marries Paltiel, who is exactly the opposite kind of man than David—urbane and polished, a nobleman.

We don't hear from Michal again until after her father and most of his family die in battle, and David is about to be declared king over all Israel, his ambitions near complete fulfillment. In order to placate the northern tribes, Saul's loyalists, enabling them to declare their fealty to David, the young monarch needs to reestablish his connection to Saul's royal family.

So David sends Abner, who had been Saul's commander-in-chief, to fetch back Michal, "to whom I became engaged at the price of one hundred foreskins of the Philistines" (2 Sam. 3:14). Michal is not consulted. She is after all David's property, since he paid for her. Abner takes Michal forcibly from her new husband, who follows along after them, weeping helplessly. Abner turns and orders Paltiel to go home. What would a husband do if facing a troop of seasoned soldiers taking his wife away? Paltiel, intimidated and demoralized, turns around and heads for home. The soldiers take Michal and deposit her in the new king's harem.

We now come to the part of the story that is included in the common lectionary. Israel here celebrates the return of the Ark into its possession—the Ark was the holiest object in Israel's religion, as is the host for Catholics or the Bible for some Protestants.

David feels joy at the prospect of bringing the Ark into his own possession and control, thus solidifying his authority over Israel. He also takes on new powers the day the Ark enters Jerusalem. By his actions he assumes control of Israel's religion as high priest—he offers animal sacrifice for the nation and gives the people the ritual priestly blessing. Ironically, when Saul acted like a priest, he (David's predecessor and Michal's father) had been condemned and ultimately driven from office by Samuel. The only apparent objection to David's activity is from Michal, and for a very different reason.

Now David dances ecstatically in front of the procession, bringing the Ark through the gates of Jerusalem, David's city, in a priestly undergarment. It is possible that his wild gyrations occasionally exposed a royal buttock, or perhaps some other private part. After dismissing the people, David returns home to a withering blast of his wife's sarcasm: "How the king of Israel honored himself today, uncovering himself today before the eyes of his servants' maids, as any vulgar fellow might shamelessly uncover himself!" (2 Sam. 6:20).

The following marital argument drips with sarcasm, hostility, and wounding venom. David's response:

> "It was before [YHWH], who chose me in place of your father and all his household, to appoint me as prince over Israel. . . . I will make myself yet more contemptible than this, and I will be abased in my own eyes; but by the maids of whom you have spoken, by them I shall be held in honor." (2 Samuel 6:21-22)

Michal maligns David for his inferior breeding and his coarse, low-class behavior. But David reminds her of her father's fate and her corresponding decline in status. The king demonstrates a complete awareness of the effect his little dance was having on his audience—David functions as his own best press agent.

David gets the last word in the argument, of course. And further, the narrator tells us that Michal never bore children, which reduced her to the lowest status in the harem's chain of authority. She was shamed publicly.

78

We today might think that her barrenness was a result of her refusal to sleep with the king, but possibly it is the result of his refusal to sleep with her. Some might suggest God's judgment on her for interfering with YHWH's intention to bless God's beloved servant, David. David's history with women is not admirable. In this case he married a woman because he wanted to be the king's son-in-law. Other such common motivations will mark his relationships in the future.

Retelling the Story

Barton stood in the hallway beside the green table where Mary had left the letter. No one had moved it since the day it arrived two weeks earlier. The periodic click of the furnace blower and the surge of warm dry air were the only sounds in the cold silence of the January afternoon. Barton stood without moving before the table and the long envelope with its bold insignia. The printed name of his wife stood out black and sharp against the thick white of the paper. He stared at the clear letters of their address, and thought of how suddenly the command had come.

Only two weeks ago, they had been doubled with laughter, talking about how the veins on Uncle Jake's forehead would bulge when he saw Uncle George again after all these years. Barton's family reunion was finally taking place after being deferred for six years. The family would be together, and everyone would meet Mary. Their wedding had been small and at a great distance from his home, and now there would be the chance for aunts, cousins, uncles, and even Great-Granddad William to meet Barton's wife, Mary. She had been looking forward to her natural place of honor among these hardworking people of whom her husband was so proud.

They had other plans, of course. Evenings over easy spaghetti dinners and candlelight, they arranged and rearranged financial plans until they were in tears, trying to find a way on his income from the plant and hers from teaching at the tech school to make a down payment on a house. But then there was some extra money from Mary's weekends with the Reserves. Mary had hopes of developing some marketable skills, as she liked to call them. How exactly she would use her experience as a weekend helicopter pilot was uncertain, but she was enjoying her new-found competence as well as the money. Barton was proud of her success and smiled with pleasure as she propped herself up on the sofa at night with the heavy, indexed, color-coded manual.

> The rabbis have many good things to say about Saul's daughter Michal. They note, for instance, that she took care of her sister Merab's five orphaned sons. She took them into her house and raised them as if they were her own. (Ginzberg IV, p. 116)

Yes, they were going to have that front door; the laundry; and one day, baby toys. And there would be evenings to talk it all over, to argue with each other, and to reconcile.

The blower switched on again. The sound brought Barton back into the afternoon. He turned away from the table and walked into their sparse living room. He did not sit in either of the dark chairs or on the old patterned sofa Mary had brought with her from her single days. He was trying to hear her coming in at the door, trying to hear the turn of the lock and her greeting whistle as she tumbled in the narrow hallway. Foolishly, he expected to see her around the corner pulling off her coat and smiling at him with her brown eyes and faint dimple. There was no sound of entry, only a thump as the blower switched off.

The dry air, the warm vents, made Barton think of the vast stretches of sand where Mary was now. The heat. The grit. The wind. All so different from their suburban apartment with the ice along the railing. How could this be? They never expected a war. They never imagined that Mary would take her helicopter to Saudi Arabia to change a desert shield into a desert storm.

In addition to her devotion to her sister's children, Michal was a very religious person. The rabbis say that though women were not required to wear phylacteries (small black boxes containing Scripture passages worn on the upper left arm and the forehead and attached with leather straps), Michal wore them. (Ginzberg IV, p. 117)

They had been naive, utterly naive. Barton ran his hand along the back of the faded flowers on the sofa, his head shaking. They had talked vaguely about defending and helping with disasters and had complained about the time away on weekends. They had made satisfied statements about serving one's country. Life was suddenly a scramble. Would he go to the reunion alone? Had she signed all the papers she needed to? What about canceling those appointments? Did she have addresses? Whom to say good-bye to? No, she had not written a will. She should leave a will.

Barton sat on the far side of the sofa, brought the blue fringed pillow across his chest and held it lightly at first, then more firmly. He had not heard from her yet. Her destination was secret, her whereabouts to him unknown. He was still waiting and knew he would wait longer.

He had driven her to the base and parked at the end of the lot. They had been unable to speak the whole way out from town. They sat in the cold car. Mary stared straight ahead as her fingers worked the lining of her coat, up and down, up and down. Barton's gaze was fixed on the bulky planes lined up for troop transport. They sat like burly squat barrels that had inexplicably sprouted dark wings.

He turned to look at her. "I love you," he was saying, and the words came back to him in a gentle echo, "I love you." He could hear her voice, but her brown eyes, her moving lips, blurred in the swell of his tears. Hot, they filled his eyes to the rim and washed over, bringing her suddenly back into focus.

"I don't want to go. I don't want to leave you. We have plans. We have our dreams."

"You are being taken from me, and there is nothing either of us can do. This is bigger than we are."

Barton had followed her all the way to the gate. He grappled with her duffel and hugged her among the dozens of families clustered by the entrance. And then she was gone.

The furnace click and hum intruded on his memory, and without warning the sobs shook his body.

"But her husband went with her, weeping after her all the way."

For many years after she chided her husband for dancing before the Ark, Michal could have no children. One story tells that when she was finally blessed with a child of her own, she died in childbirth. (Ginzberg IV, p. 177)

David Escapes from Saul

Saul, who is consumed by hatred of David, sends the young David flee-ing for his life.

The Story

That same day, when Saul had fin-ished talking with David, he kept him and would not let him return any more to his father's house, for he saw that Jonathan had given his heart to David and had grown to love him as himself. Jonathan and David made a solemn compact because each loved the other as dearly as himself. Jonathan stripped off the cloak and tunic he was wearing, and gave them to David, together with his sword, his bow, and his belt.

David succeeded so well in every venture on which Saul sent him that he was given command of the fighting forces, and his promotion pleased all ranks, even the officials round Saul.

At the homecoming of the army and the return of David from slaying the Philistine, the women from all the cities and towns of Israel came out singing and dancing to meet King Saul, rejoicing with tambourines and three-stringed instruments. The women as they made merry sang to one another:

'Saul struck down thousands,
   but David tens of thousands.'
Saul was furious, and the words ran-kled. He said, 'They have ascribed to David tens of thousands and to me only thousands. What more can they do but make him king?' From that time forward Saul kept a jealous eye on David. . . .

On his return from the pursuit of the Philistines, Saul learnt that David was in the wilderness of Engedi. Tak-ing three thousand men picked from the whole of Israel, he went in search of David and his followers to the east of the Rocks of the Mountain Goats. There beside the road were some sheepfolds, and nearby was a cave, in the inner recesses of which David and his men were concealed. Saul came to the cave and went in to relieve him-self. David's men said to him, 'The day has come: the LORD has put your enemy into your hands, as he promised he would. You may do what you please with him.' David said to his men, 'God forbid that I should harm my master, the LORD's anointed, or lift a hand against him. He is after all the LORD's anointed.' So David reproved his men and would not allow them to attack Saul. He himself got up stealthily and cut off a piece of Saul's cloak; but after he had cut it off, he was struck with remorse.

Saul left the cave and went on his way; whereupon David also came out

82

of the cave and called after Saul, 'My lord king!' When Saul looked round, David prostrated himself in obeisance and said to him, 'Why do you listen to those who say that David means to do you harm? Today you can see for yourself that the LORD put you into my power in the cave. Though urged to kill you, I spared your life. "I cannot lift my hand against my master," I said, "for he is the LORD's anointed." Look, my dear lord, see this piece of your cloak in my hand. I cut it off, but I did not kill you. This shows that I have no thought of violence or treachery against you, and that I have done you no wrong. Yet you are resolved to take my life. May the LORD judge between us! But though he may take vengeance on you for my sake, my hand will not be against you. As the old proverb has it, "One wrong begets another"; yet my hand will not be against you. Against whom has the king of Israel come out? What are you pursuing? A dead dog? A flea? May the LORD be judge and decide between us; let him consider my cause; he will plead for me and acquit me.'

When David had finished speaking, Saul said, 'Is that you, David my son?' and he burst into tears. He said, 'The right is on your side, not mine: you have treated me so well; I have treated you so badly. You have made plain today the good you have done me; the LORD put me at your mercy, but you did not kill me. Not often does a man find his enemy and let him go unharmed. May the LORD reward you well for what you have done for me today! I know now that you will surely become king, and that the kingdom of Israel will flourish under your rule. Swear to me now by the LORD that you will not exterminate my descendants

and blot out my name from my father's house.' David swore this on oath to Saul. Then Saul went to his home, while David and his men went up to their fastness. . . .

Abishai said to David, 'God has put your enemy into your power today. Let me strike him and pin him to the ground with one thrust of the spear. I shall not have to strike twice.' David said to him, 'Do him no harm. Who has ever lifted his hand against the LORD's anointed and gone unpunished? As the LORD lives,' David went on, 'the LORD will strike him down; either his time will come and he will die, or he will go down to battle and meet his end. God forbid that I should lift my hand against the LORD's anointed! But now let us take the spear which is by his head, and the water-jar, and go.' So David took the spear and the water-jar from beside Saul's head, and they left. The whole camp was asleep; no one saw him, no one knew anything, no one woke. A deep sleep sent by the LORD had fallen on them.

Then David crossed over to the other side and stood on the top of a hill at some distance; there was a wide stretch between them. David shouted across to the army and hailed Abner, son of Ner, 'Answer me, Abner!' He answered, 'Who are you to shout to the king?' David said to Abner, 'Do you call yourself a man? Is there anyone like you in Israel? Why, then, did you not keep watch over your lord the king, when someone came to harm your lord the king? This was not well done. As the LORD lives, you deserve to die, all of you, because you have not kept watch over your master the LORD's anointed. Look! Where are the king's spear and the water-jar that were by his head?' . . .

Saul said, 'I have done wrong; come back, David my son. You have held my life precious this day, and I will never harm you again. I have been a fool, I have been sadly in the wrong.' David answered, 'Here is the king's spear; let one of your men come across and fetch it. The LORD who rewards uprightness and loyalty will reward the man into whose power he put you today, for I refused to lift my hand against the LORD's anointed. As I held your life precious today, so may the LORD hold mine precious and deliver me from every distress.' Saul said to David, 'A blessing on you, David my son! You will do great things and be triumphant.' With that David went on his way and Saul returned home.

Comments on the Story

The Bible accuses Saul of being irrational, but he shows considerable reason and planning when he tries to kill David. When Saul and David return from battle, the women, showing great political insight as well as their enthusiasm, chant:

> Saul has killed his thousands;
> David, his tens of thousands.

David has become so popular in the royal court of Saul that he overshadows Saul's reputation as king.

Saul believes that David is about to replace him, and he is right. The narrator, clearly favoring David, however, highlights Saul's irrational, paranoid activity. Saul tries to arrange a marriage for David with his daughter, in order to have an occasion to destroy him. David, while innocently playing music for the king, is attacked. The king hurls a spear at the young musician, trying to pin him to the wall.

And later, when David is a fugitive, Saul seems to realize how groundless are his accusations. He apologizes to David and calls him "son." There are two versions of David's encounter with Saul in the Judean wilderness, when David was fugitive (see 1 Samuel 24 and 26). In both, Saul had led an expedition into Judah to seek out David and to capture him for his supposed opposition to Saul's authority.

The ancient model of the warrior is one who is always watchful. No one can sneak up on a warrior without being discovered. The warrior in modern films often appears as the international spy, more James Bond than Rambo or the hero of martial arts films. In our story here, David comes upon a helpless Saul in two separate accounts. In one Saul has gone into a cave to relieve himself, to have a little privacy, and David's captain says, "Now is your chance to get rid of Saul once and for all." In the other account, poor Saul is fast asleep. David cuts off a bit of his clothes, takes some personal items, and stands a safe distance away. He challenges Saul from that distance and demonstrates that while he could have killed the sleeping king he did not.

We may laugh about Saul's vulnerability, the great king caught in such an awkward and revealing situation, but there is something tragic and sadly moving about the crazed, paranoid king in his moments of lucidity. He overflows with love for David and regret for his treatment of his young friend. On occasion, though, he goes mad again and tries to kill the imagined enemy. The enemy in this case was his own mind. David doesn't take advantage of the king's vulnerability. He simply stays out of Saul's way until the king dies in battle.

No matter what you feel about Saul, his death lends him a certain majesty that is denied him in life. He is old and tired, and his intense efforts to destroy David have worn him down. Now he faces the most decisive battle of his life. The Philistines are assembled to finish off this upstart king once and for all. Further, the Philistines feel that they have an ally in David, who is now settled with his family in Philistine territory, under their protection. They believe that they will overthrow Saul and place their puppet David in his place. The Philistines are confident and prepared to expend the necessary resources to eliminate Israel once and for all. The modern echoes of this sentiment in that same part of the world are chilling when we read the newspapers and watch the TV news.

Saul faces this battle alone. Samuel is dead, and David is hiding in the Philistine camp. The loss of his oldest and most trustworthy friends (although they were often unkind to him) disturb Saul less than the loss of God. YHWH has closed him in and will not speak to Saul by any of the accustomed means: not through dreams, not by prophets, not by sacred dice. In each case the message would be either obscure or entirely absent.

Previously, Saul had allowed the priests to persuade him to eliminate their religious competitors, the popular mediums and necromancers. Their activity was banned under penalty of death. But now, in Saul's despair he has his servants find him a medium (known in literature as "the witch of Endor") to call up Samuel for him.

We are surprised to discover that the medium can successfully call up Samuel, who delivers to the hapless king a death blow. He says, "[YHWH] will give Israel along with you into the hands of the Philistines; and tomorrow you and your sons shall be with me; [YHWH] will also give the army of Israel into the hands of the Philistines" (1 Sam. 28:19). How could Saul go on, after having heard that?

Still he fights the next day and faces his death with courage. He is wounded and falls on his sword to commit suicide before the Philistines can torture and ridicule him. There is great dignity and stature here. If Saul cannot live as a king, he will surely die as one.

The death of Saul must be told with great sympathy and sadness. We must be made to care deeply about him and the tragedy of his life—the waste and lost potential. If he had been king in an easier time he would have been a great king. Circumstances overcame him, however, and drove him mad. But often we judge biblical characters by their end, their final moments. If we judge Saul that way, we can admire him for his failed greatness.

To the end he was an irrational man seeking more and more irrational means to achieve his end, but his end always was to retain power and ensure that his chosen heir would succeed him. Any dynastic ruler would want the same thing, David included.

David runs for his life from his king, and he hides in his own territory. This must have been the happiest time in David's life, camping in the woods, sleeping in caves, traveling at night with a few trusted soldiers, able to throw his weight around, not answerable to a king or bureaucracy. When David became king, his encumbrances and difficulties grew while his happiness diminished.

Retelling the Story

Saul, you will never know that I saw your suffering. You are dead. Your anointed head cut off, your weapons scattered, your embattled body nailed to a wall. Saul! Saul! What a crumbling! What a shattering! You who once wept and called me son. You who gave me your bright armor. With zealous hands you arranged your soft tunic on my shoulder. You eagerly buckled the sword from your side to my own. At first you would not let me go. You brought me into your court and dressed me in fine linen, and you lay in rapture as songs sprang from my harp.

I saw all your glory. I saw what you lost. I was a boy, and my eyes were wide as I watched the generals clamor in to report the news of battle. Their

After viewing the irrational behavior of Saul, David told God that all of creation had been well formed with the exception of people driven to madness. On hearing this, God told David that there would come a time when he would wish to be mad. Sure enough, when David was running from Saul's wrath he went to the king of the Philistines, Achish, to ask for help. Now, it just so happened that Goliath's brothers were the king's bodyguards, and they plotted to kill David. They told the king that since David had defeated the Philistines' hero, he was therefore seeking to claim the throne from Achish. Hearing this, David prayed to God that he might appear to be insane. When Achish saw David's irrational behavior, Achish said, "Don't I have enough fools and mad folk in my realm? Take this madman away." So David escaped both Saul and Achish with God's help. That is the reason, the rabbis say, that the psalm says: "I will bless the Lord at *all times*." That includes times fraught with madness. (Ginzberg IV, pp. 89-90) hard bodies shone with sweat, and their spears rattled and clanged in the outer places. Then they bowed to you. They inclined their heads to you. They listened when you spoke. The wise men consulted and brought you their words. Your court was a place of scarlet and rich embroidery. The young women danced, their dresses spangled with jewels of gold. You had killed your thousands defending Israel from enemies. The tambourines shook, and the trumpets rang out. You were the king all Israel had cried out for. You were the Lord's anointed one.

And then one day I saw you for the first time preparing for an important emissary to the court. Your hand trembled as you reached for the scroll beside you. As you hurried to gather your robe, your arm became entangled, and the fabric tore. You swung around awkwardly, stumbling, your teeth set and grinding, your jaw rigid. You lost your balance and fell hard against the couch. Servants rushed to you, but you threw them off growling and pushing. They crept back, trying to smooth the robes. You yelled at them to leave. And when they had gone, you turned your face away and your shoulders shook.

And then I remember the stories of how you had come to this court and this vast array of armies. You had come from the smallest family of the smallest tribe of Israel, but you were tall and ripe with brawn and lifeblood. They spoke of you as a simple man, concerned for your father's worries and ready to search out the donkeys when they were lost. They told of how you were anointed at the edge of town after sleeping your last night as an unburdened man alone on the roof of a house. You were one man beneath the unrelenting clamor of Israel for a king. How your heart must have beaten when Samuel spoke those words telling you that the Spirit of the Lord would take possession of you, and that you would become another man.

> David once complained to God that many creatures that were crafted by the divine hand seemed so useless--the spider, for example. Even its web is so fragile that it cannot possibly serve a useful purpose. Later, however, when Saul was in hot pursuit, David hid in a cave. Saul's soldiers were searching every nook and cranny of the surrounding area. Seeing this, God sent a spider to spin a web across the opening of the cave. When the soldiers started to enter the cave where David was hidden Saul pointed to the spider web and told them that if anyone had entered the cave the web would not still be intact. So something as apparently fragile and useless as a spider web turned Saul and his soldiers away and saved David's life. (Ginzberg IV, p. 90)

You were torn suddenly without time for a backward glance, torn from the hills and houses of your young manhood and cast among prophets. You would be the flesh between the kingship of God and the kingship of men. You were to be the first, thrust out onto the plains of a struggling Israel.

We shared that stunning change, you and I. One day we were simple boys among asses and sheep, and the next we were princes and warriors. And did you know that new heart within you? Did the rapt dancing make your heart's beating more familiar? Were you overwhelmed? Did your modesty overtake you? Is that why you hid in the baggage when they came for you shouting, "Long live the king!"?

You had known victory. You had days of authority when your actions were as swift as eagles and stronger than lions. Nahash had fallen under your spear. Your victories brought celebration and joy. And then the people and the Spirit of God began to drift away, and the knowledge of rejection grew and rankled and pierced your once modest heart. Your destiny was impossible. You were the king the people cried for, and you were chosen by the Lord; but you were unwanted by the same people and the same God. You faltered as your purpose clouded over. Yes, you disobeyed, and you led the people to harm; but you turned and tried again and again and again. Like a desperate, drowning man, you grasped and raged, and your confusion thickened. You turned against your own son Jonathan. Your once strong heart was filled with fear. You could only be who you were, and you could only be abandoned.

And then I appeared, and the fear consumed you and the jealousy outgrew all reason. The darkness drew in close about your mind, and you were engulfed and deserted. Your spear flew out against me before you knew that it was your hand that threw it. The harp that had comforted you now haunted you. I became the son you wanted and could never have. I was with the God you had served, and you could not find God anywhere. You might avenge yourself on priests, splattering their children's blood in your vengeance, but it was over. The light had left you forever, and what else could you see but ghosts and spirits? Where else could you go but to a cave?

Saul, I never lifted my hand against you. That much you know. You went before me into the unknown realm. You went suddenly and alone. You lived out those last dreadful days with the full knowledge that your legacy had been torn from your hand.

David hated wasps and thought them even more useless than spiders. Yet, when he entered Saul's camp to prove that he could have killed the king but chose not to, he decided to take a cruse of oil from between the feet of Abner as a sign of his presence. Just as David was about to escape, Abner brought his legs together in his sleep, trapping David between his strong calves. At just that moment along came a wasp and stung Abner, making him jerk his legs apart without waking. This allowed David to escape, and he never maligned any of God's creation after that. (Ginzberg IV, pp. 90-91)

David and Jonathan

Jonathan proves his friendship with David at the risk of his relationship to Saul and even Jonathan's own life.

The Story

David made his escape from Naioth in Ramah and came to Jonathan. 'What have I done?' he asked. 'What is my offence? What wrong does your father think I have done, that he seeks my life?' Jonathan answered, 'God forbid! There is no thought of putting you to death. I am sure my father will not do anything whatever without telling me. Why should my father hide such a thing from me? I cannot believe it!' David said, 'I am ready to swear to it: your father has said to himself, "Jonathan must not know this or he will resent it," because he knows that you have a high regard for me. As the LORD lives, your life upon it, I am only a step away from death.' Jonathan said to David, 'What do you want me to do for you?' David answered, 'It is new moon tomorrow, and I am to dine with the king. But let me go and lie hidden in the fields until the third evening, and if your father misses me, say, "David asked me for leave to hurry off on a visit to his home in Bethlehem, for it is the annual sacrifice there for the whole family." If he says, "Good," it will be well for me; but if he flies into a rage, you will know that he is set on doing me harm. My lord, keep faith with me; for you and I have entered into a solemn compact before the LORD. Kill me yourself if I am guilty, but do not let me fall into your father's hands.' 'God forbid!' cried Jonathan. 'If I find my father set on doing you harm, I shall tell you.' David answered Jonathan, 'How will you let me know if he answers harshly?' Jonathan said, 'Let us go into the fields,' and so they went there together.

Jonathan said, 'I promise you, David, in the sight of the LORD the God of Israel, this time tomorrow I shall sound my father for the third time and, if he is well disposed to you, I shall send and let you know. If my father means mischief, may the LORD do the same to me and more, if I do not let you know and get you safely away. The LORD be with you as he has been with my father! I know that as long as I live you will show me faithful friendship, as the LORD requires; and if I should die, you will continue loyal to my family for ever. When the LORD rids the earth of all David's enemies, may the LORD call him to account if he and his house are no longer my friends.' Jonathan pledged himself afresh to David because of his love for him, for he loved him as himself.

Comments on the Story

Kings customarily look to their oldest sons to rule when they are gone. The prince's entire childhood and early manhood comprises his education and preparation to take over the throne. Samuel established a dynasty beginning with Saul, and Saul's chosen successor was his son Jonathan.

Jonathan's culture obligated him to submit to the authority of his father, and to betray his father to the enemy was unthinkable and treasonous. What was it that compelled Jonathan to lose faith in Saul and swear his allegiance to a man who stood to become king in his place?

Many of us can remember a time when we lost faith with one or both of our parents, when they became merely human to us. For Jonathan it was worse. He found his father impulsive and vain, and what's worse, his father often played the fool in front of everybody.

Everyone liked Jonathan, a popular and commanding figure. His first recorded military exploit was one in which his father took all the credit (1 Sam. 13:3-4). Afterward, with a bravery that bordered on recklessness, Jonathan challenged a Philistine garrison with only his armor-bearer to accompany him. They walked over to the enemy camp, located between two rocky ridges. Jonathan needed a sign that God would support him, because he recognized that "it doesn't matter how many people [YHWH] has. He can win with only a few people." His father was not so convinced of this when facing the Philistines in an earlier encounter. When the Philistines outnumbered Saul, he panicked.

Jonathan initiated a test to determine whether YHWH would allow him to overcome the superior Philistine forces. The prince and his companion would stand on lower ground and issue a challenge to the enemy platoon. If they threatened to come down to meet the two Israelites, Jonathan would stand his ground, but if they dared him to come up and meet him, the two young men would advance. It would appear that Jonathan was determined to meet the Philistines regardless of their response, YHWH only deciding the field of battle.

It must be noted, however, that two lone warriors climbing up an outcropping are at a decided disadvantage. With swords secured so that they would remain free to grab the handholds, lugging cumbersome armor and shields, these two young men would be easy pickings for the more seasoned Philistine soldiers, defending from a secured position.

Confident of divine guidance, the two men proceeded. The narrator describes what follows with minimal detail. Jonathan engages the opposition while his shield bearer finishes them off. One might assume that Jonathan met the Philistines in a narrow place where he was able to engage them one at a time. He dispatches twenty men in succession, with bravado and a carefree demeanor reminiscent of Hollywood's Errol Flynn or Indiana Jones. The larger

Philistine camp is demoralized by the news that their forward garrison has been eliminated by two Israelite men.

Saul decides to take advantage of this situation initiated by his son. Although he has consulted the priestly oracle to determine the desirability of such a course of action, time is at a premium, and before the priest can methodically determine what YHWH wills in this matter, Saul breaks off the interview and leads his men into battle. The storyteller will need to determine whether this was rash and impulsive, impious perhaps, or a rare example of Saul's kingly decisiveness. In either case, the battle turns against the Philistines, and they scatter before the Israelite advance.

Saul, perhaps feeling guilty at short circuiting the priestly oracle, commands that as part of a sacred vow all the troops must fast for the duration of the battle. The negative result of Saul's decisiveness is his propensity for making foolish decisions. The soldiers are tired and hungry, losing energy at just the time they need to pursue the chase. Perhaps this was one of those moments in history when a different choice would have changed the course of events. The Philistines ultimately caused Saul's downfall. Had he been more sensitive to the needs of his troops, would the Philistines, already demoralized and in retreat, have been neutralized?

Before the advent of refined sugar, sources of concentrated sweetness were in very short supply. Imagine the eyes of the soldiers, then, as they passed a beehive dripping with honey. They were so hungry and weak from the forced march and the tension.

The soldiers passed the hive painfully, with averted eyes. Jonathan, mounted, has not heard the restriction, and he scoops out some honey with his spear, thus providing himself a source of quick energy. The soldiers exchange fearful glances. The punishment for breaking the king's foolish vow was death.

The battle has reached a final, decisive stage and now Saul decides to complete his efforts to determine YHWH's will by means of the priestly oracle. The oracle refuses to answer.

Some comments on Israelite oracular practice might be helpful here. The priest held divinatory stones in his vest (*ephod*) that were named Urim and Thummim (pronounced Oor'-eem and Too'-meem) which literally mean "lights and perfections." Although these are two words, this does not necessarily mean that there were two stones. If there were two stones, presumedly one would indicate "yes" and the other "no."

But this would not account for "no answer." If there were four stones, two of one color would indicate "yes," two of the other "no." More commonly one would get one of each, which would be interpreted as YHWH's refusal to answer.

Alternately, the oracle would require a separate interpretive step in the process, whereby the priest would be required to "read" the oracle, providing a prophetic communication that would correspond to the configuration of the stones. In this case, YHWH's refusal to answer would pertain to some priestly check, a constraint on the priest that prevented him from accurately reading the stones.

In either scenario, YHWH refused to provide an answer to Saul's inquiry. Clearly this must be the result of some sin in the Israelite camp. The Philistines forgotten, and presumably escaping to their fortified cities to fight another day, Saul performs priestly detective work to determine the guilty culprit who is blocking YHWH's word.

Saul divides the camp into two uneven groups, the king and his son on one side and the assembled Israelite army on the other. The oracle unambiguously points to the royal family as the cause of the divine silence. A second consultation determines Jonathan as the guilty party.

Although Saul, when caught in a transgression, seeks to divert the blame to those around him, Jonathan takes full responsibility. "I have eaten the honey. I am ready to die." Some have seen a touch of irony in Jonathan's response, as if he were saying, "Are you actually going to execute me for a little bit of honey?"

If so, the irony is lost on Saul, who orders his son stoned to death, in accordance with the ancient traditions. Had Saul heard the story of Jephthah, who had his only daughter killed in obedience to a foolish vow? If so, there is no indication of hesitation or remorse.

The troops react differently. They cry out in outrage and disgust at this foolish edict, and the text says that they "ransom" Jonathan. It is certainly possible that they ransomed him with the sacrificial death of an animal, but more likely, one of their own number was sacrificed to preserve the young prince's life, a human life forfeited to preserve the king's progeny. What a horrible price to pay for Saul's stupidity!

Was this the moment that Jonathan lost faith and confidence in his father's leadership? We are told that when David joined the royal court, Jonathan immediately linked his fortunes with this rising star, and he risked his own life and royal position to protect his newfound friend. He opposed his father, risking the wrath of the unstable monarch.

With David present, Jonathan willingly takes second billing, and when David leaves Gibeah, we hear nothing of the prince. The narrator's focus is on the conflict between Saul and David. Finally, Jonathan dies, fighting at his father's side in the last tragic struggle of the house of Saul against the Philistines, in a battle that might never have happened, had Saul continued his pursuit in the hill country of Ephraim.

The storyteller might approach this story from the perspective of generational conflict, a father rigidly imposing a destiny of an unwilling son, or perhaps emphasizing Jonathan's humility and willingness to take the second place in the presence of his friend David.

Retelling the Story

The mountain fields were fresh green and laced with wildflower colors—blue chicory and white wild carrot, orange butterfly plant, black-eyed Susans, and lavender bee balm. Sheep grazed quietly among the steep hills and gray-green boulders in the old farm meadows. Turkeys gathered, white and scratching, under spreading butternut trees. The sky burned blue as a goldfinch looped from thistle to thistle. In the town, old timers gathered on the stoop of Borman's store to talk and watch the pickups and logging trucks rumble through from the south.

"Well, that boy has a rough row to hoe, a rough row to hoe," said one man, slipping a chaw into his cheek.

"Old Jake been at it again?" another asked.

"Yes, sir. Haven't you heard? 'Tother day Old Jake pointed his shot gun at his son Bill."

"Pointed it at Bill!?"

"Yes, sir. Cocked it, too."

Old Jack was often the topic of conversation among the old men at Borman's. He was a strange man, rough and hard, and he made his children's lives a misery. He worked them, taunted them. No one could ever figure him out because he was such a mix of strength and rage; he knew most things and resented even more than he knew. Yet he could tell a joke better than any farmer around.

Oh, how he worked his wife, Emmie, in that cramped mountain house. Their six children were born there. How they survived in four rooms all those years was a wonder. All the children—even the little ones—worked. There was the time they were haying on top of Green Ridge and the smallest keeled over from the heat and exertion. He had to drive her all the way back down the mountain, her head rolling from side to side like a rag doll.

Emmie planted and canned, toted and scrubbed; but Old Jake refused to have an inside bathroom even though everyone else did. The kitchen water came into the sink through a pipe run up to the spring out behind the house.

During David's reign there came one of the ten worst famines of all time. For three years he attempted to discover its cause, but to no avail. Finally, he prayed to God, and the answer came: "Was not Saul a king in Israel, yet he lies buried in the ground of another land." So David went to Jabesh-gilead and, with scholars and other important figures from Israel, gathered the remains of Saul and Jonathan. They were taken to Israel and buried in family lands belonging to the tribe of Benjamin accompanied by grieving throngs of people. After this the famine ended. (Ginzberg VI, pp. 109-10)

When Emmie died, she was worn out. Old Jack said that while she was living he never thought his wife did much. Now she was gone, he reckoned she had.

The eldest boy, Bill, took Jake's ranting worse than the others. When he tried to get new farm equipment, Old Jake called Bill a fool. Bill tried to move the junk car from the side of the pasture gate. Old Jake wouldn't hear of it. He said it had sat there for six years, and it could sit there another six. Bill would slam his fist on the kitchen table, and Old Jake would yell. For some reason, Bill stayed on. Some said Bill could see both the strength and stubbornness in his father. Others said he loved his father but just didn't know what to make of him.

Long ago, his dad had been the first to get into sheep farming, others had laughed at him. Why, no one in that area had ever raised sheep for a living. There was buckwheat and corn, turkeys and chickens, and maybe a few sheep; but not flocks of them. Old Jake had foreseen their value. He bought new breeds and built sturdy flocks. When his flocks grew, he saved the strongest lambs for breeding rather than using only the runts as others did. His ideas about marketing and transporting his sheep worked better than anyone had expected. Then he led the new sheep farmers into a tough organization that stood up against all kinds of problems. Bill's dad was a leader and brought new prosperity to families in those mountains. Still, he was a man of contradictions.

Old Jake was stubborn and jealous, and he would fly into a rage whenever Bill brought Ed over with his new ideas about sheep farming. Ed had the farm over the mountains from Old Jake, and he was succeeding with some breeding methods and had been able to keep his flocks free from disease in a way that Old Jack could neither understand nor condone. When Old Jack saw Ed on the street in town, he would spit at Ed's feet and walk on without a word.

Saul and Samuel were often at odds while alive, but the rabbis say that they are reconciled in the afterlife. God describes the dead king as "Samuel's companion in paradise" according to these sages. (Ginzberg VI, p. 269)

Bill tried to reason with his father, but there was no hope of change. Now Old Jake was accusing Ed of stealing part of his land, claiming Ed was in cahoots with the county surveyor. Old Jake swore he'd shoot the surveyor on sight for misreading the lines along the back creek. Bill stood up with his father at the assault hearing.

Only a week ago Old Jack yelled at Bill in Freeland's Restaurant over the fried chicken, shouting that Bill was no son of his, that Bill had gone over with Ed and was trying to shame his father and was trying to bring him down. In the next booth, Sarah Bennet's youngest boy started bawling and wouldn't stop. Mr. Williams the owner came over and asked Old Jake to leave. Bill sat staring at the table, his jaw knotted and his knuckles white around the handle of the coffee cup.

All of the old timers spat and pushed back on the stoop.

"Do you reckon he'll bring charges against his old man then?"

"Naw," another said, "he'll make the best of it. Always has. He'll stand by him. But you know it has to be hard for that boy to live with a father as crazy as Old Jake."

David's Lament for Saul and Jonathan

David mourns for his dearest friend, Jonathan, and the king who sought to end his life.

The Story

David raised this lament over Saul and Jonathan his son; and he ordered that this dirge over them should be taught to the people of Judah. It was written down and may be found in the Book of Jashar:

Israel, upon your heights your
   beauty lies slain!
How are the warriors fallen!
Do not tell it in Gath
or proclaim it in the streets of
   Ashkelon,
in case the Philistine maidens rejoice,
and the daughters of the
   uncircumcised exult.
Hills of Gilboa, let no dew or rain fall
   on you,
no showers on the uplands!
For there the shields of the warriors
   lie tarnished,
and the shield of Saul, no longer
   bright with oil.
The bow of Jonathan never held back
from the breast of the foeman, from
the blood of the slain;
the sword of Saul never returned
empty to the scabbard.
Beloved and lovely were Saul and
   Jonathan;
neither in life nor in death were they
   parted.
They were swifter than eagles,
stronger than lions.
Daughters of Israel, weep for Saul,
who clothed you in scarlet and rich
   embroideries,
who spangled your attire with jewels
   of gold.
How are the warriors fallen on the
   field of battle!
Jonathan lies slain on your heights.
I grieve for you, Jonathan, my
   brother;
you were most dear to me;
your love for me was wonderful,
surpassing the love of women.
How are the warriors fallen,
and their armour abandoned on the
   battlefield!

Comments on the Story

In this moving poem honoring the fallen king and his oldest son, two questions hold the storyteller's interest. First, concerning the relationship of David to Saul: Why did David appear sorry at the death of his greatest enemy, the single biggest barrier to his becoming king? And second, how might we understand the nature of the relationship of David and his best friend, Jonathan, Saul's son?

Regarding the first problem, many readers have questioned the sincerity of David's motives, crying out so publicly in an act of mourning. One cannot fail to notice that the very people David needed to win over, the northern tribes loyal to Saul, are the ones most likely to be impressed by such an open display of sorrow over the loss of King Saul.

To his credit, however, David seemed to have a high regard for anyone who had received the mantle of leadership from YHWH, regardless of their qualifications or feelings toward him. He studiously avoided any attempt to harm or overthrow the previous king, declaring that "YHWH's anointed" was off limits to human efforts at revenge. We thereby may assume that David would have mourned broadly for any king, regardless of any previous relationship.

Jonathan is another story. Although Jonathan was David's chief rival for the throne, the narrator takes great pains to establish how they loved each other in spite of David's ambition. Jonathan seemed undisturbed by David's ascendancy. Perhaps he was relieved to avoid the heavy burden and responsibility. Perhaps he knew that David was YHWH's choice. Or perhaps he simply loved David that much.

Many possible political motives exist in the relationship between David and Jonathan, but we cannot fail to be moved by the intimacy of the description of this relationship. "The soul of Jonathan was bound to the soul of David, and Jonathan loved him as his own soul. . . . Then Jonathan made a covenant with David, because he loved him as his own soul" (1 Sam. 18:1-3). And in the poem itself:

> I am distressed for you, my brother Jonathan;
> greatly beloved were you to me;
>> your love to me was wonderful,
>> passing the love of women.
>
> (2 Sam. 1:26)

Somehow, the power of these words demands that they be taken seriously on their own terms.

Certainly, it suits David politically to be on friendly terms with his chief rival; yet Jonathan often intervened in court on David's behalf, and even risked his own position as favored son by helping David escape the capital city. These acts go far beyond political favors.

What an extraordinary person was Jonathan! In spite of lifelong training, he seemed to have no ambition to be king. For him friendship was paramount, even over loyalty to his father and his father's expectations of him. He recognized David's superior ability; Jonathan believed that YHWH had chosen

David to rule, and he certainly saw David's ruthless ambition, the fire in his eyes. Jonathan gladly yielded his position and seemed relieved to be rid of it. Don't mistake this for cowardice, for we are reminded that Jonathan was his father's most decorated warrior, a soldier beloved by the entire army.

Once, when Jonathan had led the entire army to a successful encounter against the Philistines, Saul vowed that anyone who ate anything before the complete victory would be ritually executed. Jonathan, who was not aware of this vow, dipped his spear into some wild honey and ate it. When Saul found out, he ordered the execution of his son, and Jonathan was willing to die.

The people, however, insisted that Jonathan be spared, "Shall Jonathan die, who has accomplished this great victory in Israel?" (1 Sam. 14:45). They "ransomed" Jonathan, allowing him to live. There are three possibilities for this ransoming activity. Either they ransomed him by publicly opposing the king and insisting that Jonathan not be harmed. Or perhaps they offered a bull and a goat as a sacrificial substitute for Jonathan's life. Most chilling is the possibility that another human being, a volunteer from Jonathan's troop, was sacrificed in his place. We simply do not know, though human sacrifice is anathema throughout Israel's history.

Some have even suggested that David's relationship with Jonathan was sexual in nature. This appears unlikely, however; both homosexuals and heterosexuals alike will agree that there can be intimate relationships between individuals without their sleeping together or even desiring to. But they were clearly the closest of friends. Most men, especially in this day, are hard put to even imagine such close intimate relationships. A pity.

What a complicated set of feelings must have run through David's head as he sings. Saul, his enemy has been trying to kill him for years. The main obstacle standing between David and the monarchy is now out of the way. And Jonathan, his best friend, is also dead. Jonathan, too, stood between David and his goal, but that seemed never to be an issue.

There is genuine grief in David's voice as he commemorates his friend. Perhaps the grief he truly felt for Jonathan showed on his face, in his voice, the words he chose, convincing the northern elders of his sincerity concerning Saul as well.

David's sincere expressions of pain and loss began the process of bringing the pro-Saul elders into his camp. I don't know if he acted deliberately, but I wouldn't doubt it. One thing is certain: The ache in his heart for Jonathan was certainly real.

The storyteller might consider exploring the inner struggle in David, between his relief at the death of Saul and his grief at the death of Jonathan. Many times, human experience generates conflicting emotions, and the stress these conflicts cause leads to major life transformations.

Another approach might be to focus on Jonathan, telling a biography of this quiet saint, gleaning from selected portions of the longer story a chronological account. Make your own eulogy to Jonathan, or to Saul.

Retelling the Story

Tom died on a May afternoon in a third-floor apartment on the north side of the city. He died in the bed he had slept in for all those years, and Bob was with him. The rough breathing eased, stopped, and at thirty-eight years old, Tom was dead.

I had met Tom five years before. He was a poet and a nurse, and he loved to climb the White Mountains in New England. He loved the play of light among the leaves and rocks. He delighted in the rhythmic strength of his body as he moved. And he often spoke of the rapid beating of his heart as he neared the top of a ridge with the promise of a new vista, a new overlook of misty rolling mountains, vast and thick with trees. He often climbed with Bob, not so much to talk about what they saw but to see the paths and streams and circling golden hawks together.

Bob was also a nurse, but the two men were different. Tom was dark and thick in appearance; "Black Irish," he would always say. Bob was light and lean, but his electric blue eyes were as observant as Tom's deep black ones. Tom's laugh was ready and low; Bob had a smile that lit his face.

They spent their days among people in hospitals, usually those people most easily forgotten. I remember Tom's going in on holidays, Thanksgiving, and Christmas, because he said the elderly patients alone on those days felt the silence most. And Bob was the one who leapt from the lower story window and ran after the psychiatric patient. The young man stumbled blindly into traffic, and Bob darted after him. Bob was the one who caught the man and held him in his arms as the cars swerved and honked.

But what still amazes me is what Bob did when Tom became ill. By rights Bob should have left. He was not bound to stay. By rights he should have protected his career, his peace of mind, his youthful energy, his enjoyment of life. These were his right. But for two years, he gave it all up. He lived from week to week, then day to day, and finally from hour to hour.

When Jonathan realized the extent of his father's hatred of David, he was broken hearted. Saul not only threatened to kill David, his rival, but brandished his spear at Jonathan as well. Saul's violent reaction was brought on by Jonathan's defense of his friend David. when Saul had threatened David's death, Jonathan had simply asked what David had done that was so terrible that he deserved to die. This one question brought forth such rage from Saul that he was ready to attack his own son. While Saul left the table angry that night, Jonathan left filled with grief. Josephus says that Jonathan spent the night weeping for both himself and his friend. (Josephus, *Antiquities*, VI 11.10)

At first, getting to work was hard for Tom, and then he was no longer able to take public transportation. Gradually, he became weaker; the complicating illnesses erupted. The insurance ran out. The medical bills were coming in one after the other. Bob was now spending hours on the phone. Family began to call. A sister was in tears. A father was unable to speak. The hospital stays were more frequent, longer. Now the smell of hospital halls never left Bob. And then the hospital would no longer take Tom. There was a new doctor to be found. And Tom was too weak to work. He was thin and sick and despairing. Bob stayed; he did not leave.

But Tom was terrified that he would. It was a Sunday afternoon when Tom stood in the hall, leaning against the wall calling to Bob, "You will leave me. I know you will leave me. No! Please don't leave me! Please."

And who would have blamed Bob if he had? The pain was so great—too much for one person. Too much. The vomiting, the delirium, the sleeplessness, the wasting away, the wrenching "what ifs," the slow unrelenting decay . . . day after day after day.

The Bible says that David's grief was greater than Jonathan's at their parting. Josephus adds that David fell at the feet of his friend and called Jonathan the preserver of his soul. Instead of allowing his friend to humble himself in that manner, Jonathan lifted David up, and they embraced. Refusing to stand above his friend, Jonathan insisted on the mutuality of friendship, and they parted, not knowing whether they would see each other again. (Josephus, *Antiquities,* VI 11.10)

Then in May Tom came back from the hospital in the throes of his final illness. He wanted to die at home in his own room with the one who loved him. The crabapple tree on the street was blooming, and the clear light of spring played among the leaves patterning the walls. Tom had not spoken for many hours. He was curled on his side, a small shape in the large bed. And then, just before three o'clock, he turned to Bob and whispered, "I think this is it."

Bob took Tom's hand in his and said, "Tom, do you remember the mountain we used to climb years ago? We climbed to the very top and looked out. I have your hand. Come, we are going to climb this one together."

David, King of All Israel

David is acknowledged as monarch over the northern and southern kingdoms, and he moves his capital to Jerusalem.

The Story

All the tribes of Israel came to David at Hebron and said to him, 'We are your own flesh and blood. In the past, while Saul was still king over us, it was you that led the forces of Israel on their campaigns. To you the LORD said, "You are to be shepherd of my people Israel; you are to be their prince."' The elders of Israel all came to the king at Hebron; there David made a covenant with them before the LORD, and they anointed David king over Israel.

David came to the throne at the age of thirty and reigned for forty years. In Hebron he had ruled over Judah for seven and a half years, and in Jerusalem he reigned over Israel and Judah combined for thirty-three years.

The king and his men went to Jerusalem to attack the Jebusites, the inhabitants of that region. The Jebusites said to David, 'You will never come in here, not till you have disposed of the blind and the lame,' stressing that David would never come in. None the less David did capture the stronghold of Zion, and it is now known as the City of David. On that day David had said, 'Everyone who is eager to attack the Jebusites, let him get up the water-shaft to reach the lame and the blind, David's bitter enemies.' That is why they said, 'No one who is blind or lame is to come into the LORD's house.'

David took up his residence in the stronghold and called it the City of David. He built up the city around it, starting at the Millo and working inwards. David steadily grew more and more powerful, for the LORD the God of Hosts was with him.

Comments on the Story

When all the tribes of Israel acknowledged David as king, he had achieved his highest ambition—the moment he had worked toward for most of his adult life. But David's unique genius was that everyone involved believed YHWH had chosen David as an *unlikely candidate* and *through no merit of his own.* Perhaps even David believed this himself.

The two explanations for David's ascendancy, YHWH's effort and David's ambition, are interwoven and merged in the stories of David now extant. David remains "YHWH's choice," even as he skillfully manipulates his image in the minds of his people, not surprising for any leader.

It is certainly possible to tell the story taking only one of these perspectives—focus on David's ambition or on all the "miracles" that occurred in David's life, the fortuitous circumstances, that bring him to the throne. But it is more suggestive to at least consider holding the two in tension. Do not try to harmonize the divergent incidents. Rather, the storyteller may wish to alternate accounts that demonstrate one or the other perspective.

Many people may identify the turnings in David's life with their own experiences of divine guidance, but at every step the choice to follow is ours. What humans do is "all from God" *and* a result of human instrumentality.

There are two stories that attempt to explain how David began his political career. In the first, he comes to Saul's court as a musician, almost a shaman whose music provides spiritual and psychological healing to the ailing king. Whenever Saul felt severely depressed he would call for his musician, whose magical songs would drive the demons out of Saul's mind. David was a musical exorcist. As a result, he becomes Saul's close companion and confidant, until the king's unreasoned paranoia drives them apart.

In the second story, David appears first as a military hero, a young boy who defeats a giant and works his way up through the military. These two beginnings are very different—the effete artist and the macho warrior.

David marries the king's daughter (see the story about David and Michal) not because he loves her, but because "it pleased David to be the king's son-in-law." It made him, shall we say, well-connected.

There is no need to "solve" the interpretive problem presented by these two versions of the story for the audience. There is in fact no solution, if by solution we mean a way to completely harmonize the two in a single, uncontradictory chronology. The Israelites felt no great need to create such chronologies; they are a modern invention. To let go of one or the other is to lose some important element of David's ascendancy. Tell them both and let them stand as variations on the theme of David's coming to power. Simply allow the ambiguity to stand.

When David had to flee south, due to Saul's justifiable suspicion over David's ambition, David assembled a small army. They were mostly misfits and outlaws, marginalized people who had loyalty only for David, for they had never belonged to any tribe, nation, or band. They gave him a completely independent power base, neither monarchic nor tribal.

Upon the death of Saul, David took control of Judah, his home province, the strongest among the tribal league, a tribal organization that had always existed as a rival structure in Saul's Israel. And he began to plan, with some of the leading powers in the north, the destruction of Saul's family, with the exception of his offer of protection for Jonathan's handicapped son, Mephibosheth.

Now the long-awaited time had finally arrived. The elders of the northern tribes begged him to be their king. They even reminded him of their familial connection, something they had often denied: "Look, we are your bone and flesh" (2 Sam. 5:2).

We will never know for sure how many people David destroyed in his climb to the top. How many would he destroy as king to maintain his power? That story is yet to come. And yet the writer or editor of this text weaves in another story—that of David, chosen of YHWH as mystical savior of Israel. Not that the first story is the "true" one, and the second is merely propaganda; rather, they are somehow *both* true, in the complex way that we know this unusual and self-contradictory human figure—this ambitious scoundrel is *also* YHWH's chosen and blessed king.

The storyteller should keep in mind that David holds our attention primarily because of his complexity. To make him a saccharine figure or entirely sleazy is to destroy him. The storyteller can hold the tension and make David come alive by keeping in the listeners' minds the image of someone they know—perhaps even themselves.

Retelling the Story

The Bible study class had been telling stories about their church's past that evening. New members were listening to older members recall and describe people who had lived the life of that congregation long ago and not so long ago. Before their imaginations rose characters of love and dedication, of struggle and disappointment, of courage and endurance.

There was laughter as one member told of Mr. Elkard, who always snored during long sermons, but who never failed to appear on church clean-up days, rake and clippers in hand. He made sure the azaleas by the front door were

David was a powerful king with a number of advisers. Among them was Ahithophel. Reading his horoscope misled this adviser into thinking that he would be king one day. So when David's son Absalom rebelled against his father, Ahithophel joined with Absalom in the vain hope that through this rebel the throne would one day pass to him. Unfortunately for him, Ahithophel's royal ambitions proved to be his undoing. (Ginzberg IV, p. 95)

mulched, watered, and fed. Each spring their floating blooms billowed around the church's carved wooden doors like soft waves of pink, lavender, and white.

Then there was Mrs. Ronlord, whose hat grew larger and more maroon with every season and whose evenings at the homeless shelter grew in direct proportion to the size and color of her hat.

Ahitophel ended his life by hanging himself. His will included three pieces of advice for those who would follow after him. First, never oppose a person whom good fortune supports. Second, don't rebel against David or any of his successors. (Clearly good advice, considering Ahitophel's fate.) Finally, and very practically, he suggested that if Shavuot (Pentecost) happened to be a sunny day, farmers should plant wheat. Perhaps the rabbis were expressing something of the conflict they felt between the Jewish and Greco-Roman wisdom traditions when they indicated that Ahitophel was the teacher of the great Greek philosopher Socrates. (Ginzberg IV, pp. 96-97)

Someone recalled Frank Bismal, who came faithfully every Sunday, no matter what the weather or the nature of the service, and sat in the right front row. As children the speakers had marveled at Frank's uninterrupted appearance each week. His regular worship was a powerful example for them when they were children. It was only many years later that they learned that Frank was mentally still a child himself and lived in an institution near the church. "He taught me something about being steadfast," one woman reflected.

The talk swelled and swirled from one person to another until the room was peopled with the women, children, and men of that timeless body, past and present. And then someone spoke the name of Sam Namsdog, after which there was a moment or two when no one spoke.

Sam was much the same as any other member. He was an ordinary looking man, perhaps a little taller than most, not handsome, but certainly not ghastly. He laughed, worked, and pondered the mysteries of the church budget and helped wash up after potluck suppers. But he was also different from the rest, and his life had touched all who called that church their spiritual home.

Sam had a remarkable but enigmatic relationship with God. There was no doubt about that, and he was as intricately woven with passions, desires, failures, and triumphs as any human being could be. He felt fully; he thought deeply; he failed utterly; he succeeded gloriously. Through all his efforts and trials, he talked with God. He opened his heart; he wept; he listened; he changed his mind; he acted. He trusted that God's Spirit would be with him and would sustain him as he plunged eagerly into life.

When Sam and Marsha moved to the church years ago, they were not married. They lived together near the river, and people said that whenever they passed the place they could hear singing. The garden behind the house began to fill with roses and foxgloves and peonies.

There had been discussions, well arguments really, about whether such a pair should be allowed to attend the church. Weren't they a bad influence?

What about the children at church? Scripture said it was wrong. More to the point, who would tell them they couldn't come?

And then there was the great fire. Houses ignited in block after block. They flared up orange and sparkling against the thick smoke of a sky. The wind shifted beyond the river, and the church was in danger. Sam climbed the roof of the church and all night he sat, the sparks singeing the black hair on his head and arms. He sat with a hose and sprayed the roof of the church, saving it from the fire. Because their house was spared, Marsha and Sam offered beds and cooked meals to any who needed them. A few years later they married, and the whole congregation came to sing and dance and rejoice at their wedding.

In the 1960s Sam became an organizer. The city denied there were any homeless people within its limits. The gray bodies on park benches belonged to someone else. So Sam found a base of operations in a floundering downtown church. The congregation had dwindled to a meager few. The building appeared cavernous and dingy with neglect. Doors creaked. Sunday school rooms were now dusty storerooms for moldy books, broken chairs, papers, and hymnals.

Sam found a sparse upstairs room for an office, put up his photographs of Gandhi, Martin Luther King, and Mother Teresa and set to work. He used to say all good things come to those who wait, just make sure you work like hell while you wait. And he did.

He also prayed diligently and usually not very quietly. One week there was no food for the kitchen, and the doors were to open in two hours. Sam and his tiny volunteer staff stood in a circle silently and then swayed in full-bodied song. No one remembers exactly when the two vans arrived full of provisions, but everyone is certain that they arrived in time for the opening of the shelter. Before winter there was shelter and food and seven local churches involved in helping seventy-eight people the city denied existed.

Soon after this triumph, Sam broke off his friendship with Jim. They had worked closely together for years, sung tenor in the choir, planned for the church late into the night, shared family celebrations. And then Jim found the needs of his family changing. He and Linda decided, after much agonizing, to move to another church. Well, Sam was outraged, saying they were traitors, and he refused to talk to them. His friends were heartsick, bewildered, and moved on with great sadness.

After a year Sam began to see the truth in his friends' actions. What he had willfully misunderstood, he began to reconsider. He had cried out against his friends; and when he reckoned with their distress, he prayed and opened himself to seeing anew. Doing that was so like him. He approached his friends again, little by little, and found they loved him still and welcomed his return. A precious friendship had almost been lost by the raging of Sam's anger, but then a new depth to the friendship was restored.

Sam became a beloved elder of the church. The stories of his life arose often. People could not resist telling stories of both his irresistible humanity and his abiding love of God.

The Fear of the Ark

As the Ark of God is being carried to Jerusalem it begins to topple. Uzzah reaches out to steady it, and upon touching the Ark, he dies.

The Story

David again summoned the picked men of Israel, thirty thousand in all, and went with the whole army that was then with him to Baalath-judah to fetch from there the Ark of God which bore the name of the LORD of Hosts, who is enthroned upon the cherubim. They mounted the Ark of God on a new cart and conveyed it from Abi-nadab's house on the hill, with Uzzah and Ahio, sons of Abinadab, guiding the cart. They led it with the Ark of God upon it from Abinadab's house on the hill, with Ahio walking in front. David and all Israel danced for joy before the LORD with all their might to the sound of singing, of lyres, lutes, tambourines, castanets, and cymbals.

When they came to a certain threshing-floor, the oxen stumbled, and Uzzah reached out and held the Ark of God. The LORD was angry with Uzzah and struck him down for his imprudent action, and he died there beside the Ark of God. David was vexed because the LORD's anger had broken out on Uzzah, and he called the place Perez-uzzah, the name it still bears.

David was afraid of the LORD that day and said, 'How can the Ark of the LORD come to me?' He felt he could not take the Ark of the LORD with him to the City of David; he turned aside and carried it to the house of Obed-edom the Gittite. The Ark of the LORD remained at Obed-edom's house for three months, and the LORD blessed Obed-edom and his whole household.

When David was informed that the LORD had blessed Obed-edom's family and all that he possessed because of the Ark of God, he went and brought the Ark of God from the house of Obed-edom up to the City of David amid rejoicing. When the bearers of the Ark of the LORD had gone six steps he sacrificed a bull and a buffalo. He was wearing a linen ephod, and he danced with abandon before the LORD, as he and all the Israelites brought up the Ark of the LORD with acclamation and blowing of trumpets. As the Ark of the LORD was entering the City of David, Saul's daughter Michal looked down from a window and saw King David leaping and whirling before the LORD, and she despised him in her heart.

After they had brought the Ark of the LORD, they put it in its place inside the tent that David had set up for it, and David offered whole-offerings and shared-offerings before the

LORD. Having completed these sacrifices, David blessed the people in the name of the LORD of Hosts, and distributed food to them all, a flat loaf of bread, a portion of meat, and a cake of raisins, to every man and woman in the whole gathering of the Israelites. Then all the people went home.

Comments on the Story

King David lacked one thing to make his control over Israel complete. There was still somewhere out there an ornate wooden box, overlaid with gold and statuary, that we English-speakers commonly call "the Ark." The Ark was an oblong box, wider and deeper than a coffin and about as long. They overlaid it with gold, most notably a thick slab of gold that rested on the top. This was called the "Seat of Mercy," and YHWH was thought to sit on that gold slab and rule Israel from that position. Over the Ark, attached at either end, were beaten gold figures of combined human-eagle-lion figures, called cherubim. In ancient Near Eastern poetry the Canaanite god Ba'al rode through the sky on the backs of such cherubim. The Ark was usually carried by inserting poles into golden rings placed at regular intervals at the sides of the box. Only priests were allowed to carry the Ark.

It symbolized tribal unity and was believed to be YHWH's actual throne whenever he sat down to judge Israel. As long as it remained outside David's city, Jerusalem, it was a focus of power that resisted his control—the tribes could rally around this Ark, perhaps against him.

But the Ark had been held in dusty storage in Israel's western borderlands, almost forgotten for over forty years, ever since it had been captured by the Philistines and released before the reign of King Saul. Now, David brought it out from Abinadab's household and marched it in festal procession toward Jerusalem.

One of the Abinadab's sons, Uzzah, marched beside the Ark, which they had loaded onto an oxcart. Oxcarts were the trucks of the ancient world. They were made of roughhewn wood with thick wooden wheels, made of a few pieces of heavy wood, joined together and shaped in a circle. They were heavy even without cargo, and two oxen pulled it, attached by a heavy yoke that rested on their shoulders.

Uzzah's brother Ahio marched in front. Then something happened. Perhaps the cart hit a rock and was jolted. The Ark became unsteady and began to fall.

It is doubtful that Uzzah even thought about what he was doing. There are times when a thing is about to happen and one acts, without reflection. So Uzzah reached out and steadied the Ark.

How odd that the text tells us first what happens to Uzzah before it tells that he had steadied the "Covenant Box." We are meant to notice first that YHWH "burst out" against Uzzah, killing him. The violence and surprise of the attack crowd out all other impressions.

But what does it mean for YHWH to burst out against someone? Some have compared it to electrocution or cosmic death rays in modern science fiction stories. In any case, Uzzah lies dead and smoking, beside the oxcart. On top of the Ark stood, in beaten gold, the figures of two sphinx-like creatures, known as cherubim. Upon what a horrible scene they looked!

The story closes with David's horrified reaction. He expressed both anger and fear. He halted the procession immediately—it had already stopped. He named the place Perez-Uzzah ("that which attacks Uzzah" is a loose translation). David did not even mention a name or title of the Israelite God. He could not bring himself to do so. In David's conception, YHWH lurks as an aggressive demon-like figure, ready to strike out against anyone. "Uzzah's attacker" could easily be understood as the enemy of humanity. Everyone continued the journey home, disappointed and fearful.

There is another surprise in store, however. Just when you think you have YHWH figured out, and you warn people "Stay away! Dangerous!" David hears the news that Obed-edom, in whose house the Ark had now been placed, had been "blessed" by YHWH. How did YHWH bless him? We are not told specifically—perhaps with children, a bountiful harvest, or in a more general way events in his life began to work out positively. The effect is cumulative and obvious to all.

We find it incongruous that the same object that represented danger to those who had contact with it would also bring blessings to those who stayed in its close proximity. But consider how healthy and realistic is this so-called primitive notion of divine power. Many have experienced God in just such a fashion. Sometimes God's power appears dangerous, wounding as readily as it heals. Other times one shares with the psalmist the experience that "at your right hand are pleasures forevermore." C. S. Lewis had it exactly right when he described Aslan, a leonine representation of Christ, as "not a tame lion."

So David tried again to bring the box into Jerusalem. The priests and the people, David most of all, took even greater care this time, and everything went smoothly.

David danced wildly and ecstatically as he led the procession, probably for hours. As he moved, David fell into a powerful trance in which he experienced directly the presence of God—this was David's greatest moment.

But when the Ark finally came under David's control, it never again affected him so deeply. David, who always hovered between two passions—the pursuit of power and the pursuit of God—now had the Ark within the royal compound. So he pursued power more insistently. As he aged he often reminisced that he was back on that road, dancing in front of the Ark. That was the only time the power of the Ark had truly gripped him, when his pursuit of YHWH was nearly single-minded.

Retelling the Story

My friend Rivka and I have been walking through Jerusalem. Rivka is on her way to an early morning dance class, and her blue dance bag bumps against her back as we walk through the maze of little alleys up and out of the Old City. The morning light sets the domes and arches aglow as it spreads over the city's golden bricks. Scarlet flowers splash silken colored along the windows, and women in long, dark, embroidered dresses with tall bundles on their heads sweep silently past on their way to market.

From where we have climbed we can see the city's ancient gates and look out beyond to the Mount of Olives. Rivka points her slender fingers toward the rolling hills of the desert. "Out there beyond that rise," she says, "David grazed his sheep." We stop and look. In every direction are holy places. The Dome of the Rock gleams turquoise and gold. Behind the brown robes of the Brothers gathered along its wall, the Church of the Holy Sepulcher is awash in rose and white, its black spire shimmering.

We turn into the modern streets of the New City. Busy Israelis hurry past, sandals padding quickly along the stones. Armenian women, dark flowing figures, float by us. Two barefoot Arab children chatter and duck into a doorway. Off-duty soldiers in green uniforms stroll in groups of two and three. A short rabbi, his beard and side curls bobbing up and down, speaks emphatically with his hand on his listener's chest. Rivka's liquid laughter fills the golden air, "You know," she says, "Jerusalem is a letdown for some people. After all the stories they read of the Holy City, their images can be very fanciful, and really it's just a hick town with only a few movie theaters and plenty of ugly apartment buildings." She pauses, and her eyes scan the glowing city. "But I love it," she softly adds, "The light is different here. Everywhere you look the air is filled with a shimmer of gold and rose. This is the real place, not the pictures or the stories, but the Golden City itself."

> Josephus suggests that Uzzah died upon touching the Ark, even though his motives were good. Still he was not a priest and should not have been touching a holy thing. This interpretation, however, doesn't seem to have satisfied the common folk, who felt that Uzzah's death was most unjust. They honored the place where he fell and called it the Breach of Uzzah. (Josephus, *Antiquities*, VII, 4.2)

As she talks I think of how Rivka not only loves this city but she also loves to dance in it. She dances with her whole heart. Her body moves with precision, strength, and grace. When I watch her performances, I marvel at the variety of her movements. Her arms sweep and grasp. Her legs and feet effortlessly follow an invisible guide. Her eyes are bright; her energy radiates beyond her fingertips.

"What does it feel like to dance?" I ask.

Rivka's eyes sparkle, and then she laughs. "Sweat!" she says. "Dancing is flying! I am in a swirling world. With words I can express myself to you, of course. But when I dance, I am most expressive, for I am whole. The little parts of me have knit together—my mind, my spirit, my emotions, my body. And during that one present, evanescent moment and place, I lose my own awareness of myself and I soar. I have let go of observing myself, judging myself, and I am carried on the music. I am inspired. I am focused, integrated into a joyful human being.

"What a wonderful feeling," I murmur.

"Yes," she replies, "I have an irresistible drive to dance. Among human expression there is no substitute for me. I think with my body. I cannot tell you what I feel as well as I can show you. When I have thrown my whole being into the dance, as I must do to make it work, the discipline of the dance frees me to move without thinking. When I have that freedom and a physical challenge—well, I am flying. I am more fully myself than at any other time, a great thing to attain, a great thing to lose."

"And where does the experience take you?" I want to know.

She smiles and winks, "Why, to the truth."

"The truth?" I ask.

"Yes, the body never lies. That's what Martha Graham said."

We laugh together. Words can easily lie, but the body never does. Words equivocate and pretend; they explain and deny. But the exposed body has nowhere to hide, and the truth the body speaks is fully of the moment and then is gone. Nothing can be revised or edited, no time to distance oneself. The dance is a human body in one fleeting moment, whole and alive. Rivka turns down her street and calls back, "Today, today, my friend, is a good day for dancing!"

> The rabbis say that the family in whose house the Ark came to rest were so richly blessed that even the usual laws of nature were suspended for them. The women in that family had pregnancies of only two months' duration, and the children were born *six at a time*. The brief pregnancies must have been a blessing to the women but sextuplets could certainly be viewed as a burden instead of a blessing. (Ginzberg VI, p. 275)

No wonder David danced before the Lord for joy. Dancing was the only complete expression of joy possible. He leaped truth; he capered love. He was whole and radiant. May we all know for one moment what it is to dance without restraint before the Lord.

Will God Live in a House?

David wants to build a house for God, but word comes through Nathan that David is to do no such thing.

The Story

Once the king was established in his palace and the LORD had given him security from his enemies on all sides, he said to Nathan the prophet, 'Here I am living in a house of cedar, while the Ark of God is housed in a tent.' Nathan answered, 'Do whatever you have in mind, for the LORD is with you.' But that same night the word of the LORD came to Nathan: 'Go and say to David my servant, This is the word of the LORD: Are you to build me a house to dwell in? Down to this day I have never dwelt in a house since I brought Israel up from Egypt; I lived in a tent and a tabernacle. Wherever I journeyed with Israel, did I ever ask any of the judges whom I appointed shepherds of my people Israel why they had not built me a cedar house?

'Then say this to my servant David: This is the word of the LORD of Hosts: I took you from the pastures and from following the sheep to be prince over my people Israel. I have been with you wherever you have gone, and have destroyed all the enemies in your path. I shall bring you fame like the fame of the great ones of the earth. I shall assign a place for my people Israel; there I shall plant them to dwell in their own land. They will be disturbed no more; never again will the wicked oppress them as they did in the past, from the day when I appointed judges over my people Israel; and I shall give you peace from all your enemies.

'The LORD has told you that he would build up your royal house. When your life ends and you rest with your forefathers, I shall set up one of your family, one of your own children, to succeed you, and I shall establish his kingdom. It is he who is to build a house in honour of my name, and I shall establish his royal throne for all time. I shall be a father to him, and he will be my son. When he does wrong, I shall punish him as any father might, and not spare the rod. But my love will never be withdrawn from him as I withdrew it from Saul, whom I removed from your path. Your family and your kingdom will be established for ever in my sight; your throne will endure for all time.'

Nathan recounted to David all that had been said to him and all that had been revealed.

Comments on the Story

Modern people don't usually believe a prophet can make a mistake, especially a so-called good or genuine prophet. Nathan was David's closest adviser, a "prophet" who spoke on behalf of YHWH. When David stole another man's wife and murdered the husband, Nathan was the only person in David's court who had the courage to confront him.

But Nathan makes a colossal blunder in this narrative. David succeeds so astonishingly in establishing his kingdom and expanding his influence, that now he needs something to do. David decides to build an ornate temple, a fixed permanent building to house the Ark, and by extension, a house for YHWH.

Nathan thinks this is a great idea and gives David YHWH's blessing and strong approval on the project. David takes this word as divine encouragement, and that is most certainly the way Nathan intends it.

Then Nathan has a dream. Prophets pay careful attention to dreams. YHWH does not want David to build a temple, but reserves that privilege for David's son, the future king of Israel.

This first prophetic error is just a preface to the main story. When Nathan reports to David his dream, the narrator makes no effort to describe David's reaction to this changed message—the same prophet had given two messages from YHWH, contradictory, the change taking place overnight.

Two reasons might account for this bewildering change. In the first, this mode of telling the story is calculated to authenticate the (forthcoming) second message from YHWH. The reasoning runs this way: If YHWH would go to such lengths to change the message, and if the prophet would risk such humiliation to set the record straight, then the second message must really be true.

Second, the prophetic failure takes the focus off Nathan with regard to the actual content of the second message. You certainly can't be sure of the prophet. The message will rise and fall on its own merits.

For some reading this account today, the notion of prophetic fallibility is troubling. Many have the notion that prophets established an unhindered link with the divine and spoke only perfectly inspired words. Most Israelites held no such illusions. There were *many* prophets saying *many* things, and an intelligent citizen would have to carefully evaluate each message. They were viewed in much the same fashion that we today must regard with suspicion whatever our media tell us, as well as messages from our politicians.

The less reflective array of Israelites would follow personalities. This practice required only one decision—whom to follow. After that it was easy—believe whatever the prophet said. However, in either case, these people took their prophets seriously. Once a message was determined to be of divine origin, God might as well have said it directly. YHWH was often quoted as saying things that, if you had been there, you would have seen were actually spoken by a popular religious figure.

Ultimately, the task of choosing an authoritative prophet became so difficult among all the choices that the entire institution collapsed on itself. But for hundreds of years, prophets were a primary source of authoritative information on the will of YHWH. But they were never considered infallible.

The second message, as it now stands in the book of 2 Samuel, is at the theological and political center of the story of David. Nathan promises from YHWH that David's dynasty will never be overthrown—David is assured that he will always have a son, grandson, and so forth on the throne in Jerusalem. Who would dare resist God by opposing the divinely appointed Davidic dynasty? Especially the prophet who proclaims it? And it is certainly curious how this intensely private session between David and Nathan becomes public and widely disseminated, incorporated in the royal chronicle.

But David and Nathan both had a sense of destiny. They believed, and their experienced confirmed, that YHWH had chosen David. Nathan is sincere when he speaks of David and his descendants.

Yet the story is clearly structured to highlight the second message and give it a great deal of rhetorical weight. In fact, both the later historical and the prophetic writings attribute enormous import to this prophecy. The fortunes of the later kings of Israel rise and fall with regard to the conformity to the standards of King David. Then when the Davidic dynasty finally does fall, the prophets speak of its coming restoration as central to the Israelite hope for the future.

Hence, this is a tremendously important passage from which we gain understanding of much of the second half of the Hebrew Bible. The message of Nathan has an immeasurable impact on later developments in Israelite, Jewish, and Christian religious ideas.

The larger historical context compels later interpreters to see the contingent nature of this affirmation of David's monarchy. The monarchy did not in fact endure forever (although four hundred years is a long time), and biblical tradents (those who pass on and fashion the religious tradition) had to scramble to explain those passages in terms of this different political reality.

So the dynasty of David becomes the model for the rule of Messiah in early Jewish and Christian thought. This messiah was to be an actual descendant of David, whom YHWH would elevate to the position held by David, his ancestor. Thus a blind beggar could shout out over the noise of the crowds, addressing a distant descendant of the Judean King: "Son of David, have mercy on me."

Retelling the Story

I am sitting in a quiet room in a small West Virginia library. I sit at a round table with four wooden chairs, and the window opens onto two broad, green mountain ridges. The sun is high, and its bright August light thins the sky to blue-white, the color of mother's milk. Tractors rake the tall grass of the field below me, leaving brown lines of hay on the thick grass.

The wall behind me is lined with genealogy books of every description. In three green volumes are the chronicles of the Scotch-Irish settlement from 1745–1800. A thick blue volume holds the *Coberly Genealogy,* and nearby is the red volume of *Loyalists in the Southern Campaign of the Revolutionary War.* There are books on the Houses of Ruddle, Harmon, and Van Deventer. One tattered brown book from 1889 gives "all the fearful record" of the Johnstown Flood. A large book with pictures tells of the ancestors and descendants of Horace and Effa Hinkle. Their ancestor John Justus Hinkle built a blockhouse, which later became the site of a colonial fort, not far from here, deep in Germany Valley.

Clans, ancestors, families, and immigrants spread out behind me in the words of their histories. They tell of the multitude of descendants, the houses of our pioneers. These people moved from country to country, then territory to territory, state to state; and they carried with them their Bibles and beliefs. Some were pastors leading small flocks scattered among the mountains. Others were worshipers, searching for freedom. Many were spiritual wanderers, often alone and in danger surrounded by a wild land. Their God traveled with them "housed in curtains." The Lord's House took shape where it could in a cabin, along a stream, or on a cliff.

Nathan told David that he would not be the one to build the Temple, but his son Solomon would have that honor. Hearing this, David changed his entire view of life. The rabbis say that thereafter when David overheard his subjects wishing that he might die so that his son could get on with building the Temple, the king's heart was filled with delight rather than fear and anger. (Ginzberg VI, p. 264)

As the land became settled and the communities grew, the Houses of the Lord began to be built in one place. The nomadic and temporary was transformed into the settled and permanent. The attachment to sacred places began to take root and flourish.

The country road leading back to Rock Creek has a sharp bend, and on the land the road embraces stands a small clapboard church. The church was built about half a century ago, and the stories of its history rise from the elders like the redolence of sweet wood fires. The land around the church is bright with hollyhocks and phlox, and the grass is cut clean and short. Ira is out every week in summer with his riding mower, and his son Aaron joins him with his weed whacker. When they finish cutting, they sit under the maple at the far side of the church. Beads of sweat cover their faces and run salty into their eyes. They think of the children who will play on the grass on Sundays, their laughter and quarrels as much a part of the morning as the sermon.

The doors of the church have just been stripped and revarnished by Mary Ann. They gleam a shiny golden brown, and Mary Ann is pleased. The doors will be ready when her daughter walks through them next month on her wedding day. Out those doors she'll walk and on to another valley in another part of the state.

Seth thinks of the doors differently, of course. Last week he watched the coffin of one of his young students carried out those doors, watched the boy's sobbing mother stumble down the church steps as she stretched out her hand after the box. The day had been too shining and blue for such a scene.

Once a month, church members gather to clean the building. They paint and scrub and hammer. They tell about when the pipes froze last winter and about the flood of '82 when the waters really did part and gushed around the church. Together they eat lunch, tired and sitting with their feet up on chairs. They know that guests will come to the church and old friends will visit, and the church will welcome them. They will be welcomed with smiles and handshakes, by the polished wood and clear windows where the mountain meadows spread in the distance.

And now recently there have been a series of financial meetings. The budget must be reassessed and balanced, and there is new insurance to consider. The church must be appraised. The board of trustees has been taking apart the line items and looking at expenses. There are heating and electric bills, the new roof, and termite inspection. And what is the value of this place? How is it to be assessed in their hearts as well as on the financial worksheets?

> The reason David was not allowed to build the Temple was that he had shed so much blood by violence during this life. Anyone responsible for so many deaths could not build a House of God. Some sages even go so far as to say that because David was a violent man all his life he never had a good night's sleep, but was plagued by nightmares all his days. (Ginzberg VI, p. 264)

Shelter and renewal are here. Here is a long history of a people worshiping God. They have stood together with trouble surrounding them. They have lost members and have found new ones. Easter singing has poured out from here, and baptisms have brought tears of joy to parents who have waited long for new life. Where is this building's worth? How will it be determined? As the people care for the walls and roof, as they share their time to listen and pray, as they give their money to this home, it becomes part of who they are. With their living and their presence, this empty structure is transformed into a sacred place.

David and Bathsheba

*David sees Bathsheba, wants her for his own, and is willing to have her
husband killed to get her.*

The Story

At the turn of the year, when kings go out to battle, David sent Joab out with his other officers and all the Israelite forces, and they ravaged Ammon and laid siege to Rabbah.

David remained in Jerusalem, and one evening, as he got up from his couch and walked about on the roof of the palace, he saw from there a woman bathing, and she was very beautiful. He made enquiries about the woman and was told, 'It must be Bathsheba daughter of Eliam and wife of Uriah the Hittite.' He sent messengers to fetch her, and when she came to him, he had intercourse with her, though she was still purifying herself after her period, and then she went home. She conceived, and sent word to David that she was pregnant.

David ordered Joab to send Uriah the Hittite to him. Joab did so, and when Uriah arrived, David asked him for news of Joab and the troops and how the campaign was going, and then said to him, 'Go down to your house and wash your feet after your journey.' As he left the palace, a present from the king followed him. Uriah, however, did not return to his house; he lay down by the palace gate with all the king's servants. David, learning that Uriah had not gone home, said to him, 'You have had a long journey; why did you not go home?' Uriah answered, 'Israel and Judah are under canvas, and so is the Ark, and my lord Joab and your majesty's officers are camping in the open; how can I go home to eat and drink and to sleep with my wife? By your life, I cannot do this!' David then said to Uriah, 'Stay here another day, and tomorrow I shall let you go.' So Uriah stayed in Jerusalem that day. On the following day David invited him to eat and drink with him and made him drunk. But in the evening Uriah went out to lie down in his blanket among the king's servants and did not go home.

In the morning David wrote a letter to Joab and sent it with Uriah. In it he wrote, 'Put Uriah opposite the enemy where the fighting is fiercest and then fall back, and leave him to meet his death.'. . .

When Uriah's wife heard that her husband was dead, she mourned for him. Once the period of mourning was over, David sent for her and brought her into the palace; she became his wife and bore him a son. But what

David had done was wrong in the eyes of the LORD.

The LORD sent Nathan the prophet to David, and when he entered the king's presence, he said, 'In a certain town there lived two men, one rich, the other poor. The rich man had large flocks and herds; the poor man had nothing of his own except one little ewe lamb he had bought. He reared it, and it grew up in his home together with his children. It shared his food, drank from his cup, and nestled in his arms; it was like a daughter to him. One day a traveller came to the rich man's house, and he, too mean to take something from his own flock or herd to serve to his guest, took the poor man's lamb and served that up.'

David was very angry, and burst out, 'As the LORD lives, the man who did this deserves to die! He shall pay for the lamb four times over, because he has done this and shown no pity.'

Nathan said to David, 'You are the man! This is the word of the LORD the God of Israel to you: I anointed you king over Israel, I rescued you from the power of Saul, I gave you your master's daughter and his wives to be your own, I gave you the daughters of Israel and Judah; and, had this not been enough, I would have added other favours as well. Why then have you flouted the LORD's word by doing what is wrong in my eyes? You have struck down Uriah the Hittite with the sword; the man himself you murdered by the sword of the Ammonites, and you have stolen his wife. Now, therefore, since you have despised me and taken the wife of Uriah the Hittite to be your own wife, your family will never again have rest from the sword. This is the word of the LORD: I shall bring trouble on you from within your own family. I shall take your wives and give them to another man before your eyes, and he will lie with them in broad daylight. What you did was done in secret; but I shall do this in broad daylight for all Israel to see.' David said to Nathan, 'I have sinned against the LORD.' Nathan answered, 'The LORD has laid on another the consequences of your sin: you will not die, but, since by this deed you have shown your contempt for the LORD, the child who will be born to you shall die.'

After Nathan had gone home, the LORD struck the boy whom Uriah's wife had borne to David, and he became very ill.

Comments on the Story

The popular stories are the most difficult to retell. Even in today's barely biblically literate culture, the tale of the adulterous king who does away with his lover's husband remains familiar. The story begins with a king home alone in his palace at a time when most of the male members of his court were engaged in battle. Should he have been fighting? Another tale of David tells that he wanted to go into battle, but his generals talked him out of it because his royal person was too important to risk. Is that the situation here?

Although it is usually admirable to avoid violence, in David such choices represented a kind of royal boredom and left him with nothing to do. He saw a beautiful woman bathing on her roof across from the palace, and he desired her. Wealthy people in the ancient world used their roofs to cool off in the summer. These roofs were flat and were festooned with makeshift tents to shield them from the sun. When it was hot, people ate on their roofs and slept up there too. Apparently they also took baths on the roof.

Was Bathsheba deliberately trying to attract David? She would certainly have found it a formidable social advancement to sleep with the king. Or was she a victim of a king whose least whim is law, and whose servants and soldiers would get him anything or anyone he wants and kill anyone who stands in his way? The writer here does not explore Bathsheba's motivation, only David's. The rest, as they say, is history. Bathsheba conceives a child, and David tries to conceal his involvement. He is in a difficult position—on the one hand he is a king and can do whatever he pleases. But he is (in theory, at least) submissive to YHWH's laws, which happen to forbid adultery (sleeping with someone who is bound in marriage to another). So it wouldn't be helpful to his reputation (and perhaps his conscience) if this affair became common knowledge.

Most kings in the ancient world embody in their own persons the law of the land. There is no higher authority than the will of the king, and no one would dream of contradicting the king on affairs of state. In those cultures, however, no distinction was made between affairs of state and the personal affairs of the king. David as king of Israel suffered under significantly greater restraints.

David is portrayed as being cold-blooded here, and it is one of his worst moments. He calls for Bathsheba's husband, Uriah, and arranges for him to sleep with his wife. Was Bathsheba in on the plot? Again we are not told. The narrator clearly looks over David's shoulder and ignores Bathsheba's perspective here.

But Uriah refuses: " 'The ark and Israel and Judah remain in booths; and my lord Joab and the servants of my lord are camping in the open field; shall I then go to my house, to eat and to drink, and to lie with my wife?' " (2 Sam. 11:11). Such loyalty is infuriating. David proceeds to get him drunk, but Uriah still refuses to visit his wife. David can't understand it. Is the implication that he always sent for one of *his* wives or concubines whenever he got drunk?

Finally, the king sends Uriah back to the battle with a sealed note, instructing his general to put Uriah in the front line and then pull back, leaving him defenseless against enemy arrows. Although David was quick to kill his enemies, whether personal (the messengers of the deaths of Saul and Jonathan) or national, we have recorded no other instance where he killed a loyal officer for personal reasons. Such cold-blooded behavior toward one of his own is clearly uncharacteristic.

Joab, the general, obeyed, but lost some other soldiers in the process—what today military leaders might call "collateral damage." He knew David would be angry, so he sent careful instructions to the messenger to first speak of the defeat and then when David began to rage, to say, "Uriah the Hittite, your servant, is also dead."

How the messenger marveled at the rapid change in David's mood! Whereas before his fury at Joab's strategic and costly blunder was just beginning to rise, now he was calm and understanding: "Do not let this matter trouble you, for the sword devours now one and now another" (11:25). As if it were all by chance!

David was off the hook. He had gotten away with murder, which must have been an exhilarating experience, but at that moment a part of his soul died.

The night before Nathan confronted David, was the prophet reluctant? Did he argue with God? Did he say, "God, if I speak plainly to David, he'll kill me. I'll never get away with it." Nathan devised a brilliant plan. "I'll tell him a story that will offend his sense of justice." David still took pride in his role as defender of the poor and powerless, the widows and the orphans. Nathan was well aware of a particular widow David was comforting at that very moment, for after the period of mourning, David quickly married Bathsheba and brought her into the palace as his favorite wife.

Nathan told David a story. "A certain man had a lamb he cherished, cared for in his house, and treated as his own child. Another wealthy man had many livestock. When a visitor came to the wealthy man, rather than part with his own property, he requisitioned the poor man's lamb, slaughtered it, and made a feast."

If the story were seen as a parallel to David's situation, David's crime would appear to be merely theft of property, a crime of greed and stinginess. Could Nathan have so crassly regarded the personhood of Bathsheba as another man's livestock? More likely, it was David's sense of justice that Nathan stirred with this story, putting David in the proper frame of mind to receive correction, for it is not an easy or a common thing for kings to take criticism.

David declared that the rich man who stole the poor man's sheep should pay back fourfold. It is interesting to consider the possibility that he thereby determined his own punishment, for four of his own sons died untimely deaths, as had Uriah. But probably more important is Nathan's prophecy of discord and division, which would tear his family apart. Such divisions and hatred characterized the second portion of David's reign. David found himself successful in foreign policy, but completely out of control in his own home.

How could David tell his sons to behave themselves when what he had done became common knowledge in the court? David no longer had any moral authority. This can happen when a person's religious and political identities become fused, so that the will of the king is equivalent to God's will. It is frightening what a king is capable of doing under such circumstances.

So many of the stories of David that were part of our childhood picture him in a saintly fashion. The tradition of portraying David in the best light goes all the way back to biblical times. David became for the Deuteronomic historian the standard by which all of the later kings were judged. Most scholars feel that the depth of his repentance and his intense, though stormy, relationship with YHWH earned him the honor of being considered Israel's greatest king. Perhaps they are correct.

But this story must be included in any account of David's life, though it is thoroughly reprehensible. This story makes the claim that there are consequences to actions. It doesn't matter who you are. The worse the actions, the writer claims, the worse the consequences, whether you are king or peasant. This theological idea will be dramatically challenged, though, by later events in the historical and theological development of Israel.

Retelling the Story

I am an old woman. I have seen much of life, much of tragedy and suffering. Yet I never expected to see what I have seen, to hear what I have heard. I have been with my mistress many years. I never thought to see her in such distress and turmoil.

Before I go further, you must understand that my mistress is very beautiful. Yes, yes, I have seen much of this world. But every time I look at my mistress, I am amazed all over again. I have watched her sit in front of her polished mirror with tears trembling along the rims of her eyes. When a woman is beautiful, it is hard for her to

> After the young David had killed the Philistine giant Goliath, he needed help to take off the dead soldier's gigantic armor. The rabbis say that Goliath wore several suits indicating that his fear was equivalent to his size. A Hittite named Uriah stepped forward to assist David with this task. As his repayment, the Hittite was given an Israelite wife, who turned out to be a woman named Bathsheba. (Ginzberg IV, p. 88)

believe a man will love her for any reason other than her beauty and for the lust she fires in his body. She wanted to be known beyond her body. She often whispered to me, "To be known is to be loved." Her doubt had left a hole in her heart.

Now, the king was wicked to do what he did. About that there can be no question and no doubt about his guilt. It was not his hand that killed Uriah. No, he had other hands to do his killing, but it was his passion and his driving lust that killed that blameless warrior!

Wait, wait. How easily I blame the king. How quickly I turn against him. Give me a moment to calm myself. I am an old woman, and I do not have much time for fervor of my own. There is more to my story. You see, when he started to come to my mistress's house, she was not sure of her feelings. She was flat-

The rabbis seem very troubled at the ease with which the biblical David could take another man's wife and have the husband killed when she became pregnant with the king's child. These sages came up with several stories that attempt to clean up the king's reputation. Some suggest that it was the custom for soldiers going into battle to write for their wives decrees of divorce in case they didn't come back. In such an instance, they claim, Bathsheba was technically divorced when the king took her as his own. A second story implies that Uriah was technically guilty of a crime worthy of the death penalty by simply disobeying the king's order to spend the night with his wife. Others say that God intended for David and Bathsheba to be married from the start, but the delays and trials were due to David's rash promise to give a Hittite an Israelite wife. (Ginzberg IV, p. 103)

It seems the sages of old express the same reluctance we often feel to admitting the flaws of their leaders. The Bible, however, seems to have no qualms in portraying even the greatest leaders, warts and all.

tered, I think, by the attention of the king, but she was also greatly troubled. His persistence was not fitting.

She loved her husband. Uriah was kind, even courteous, to her. His fame was great by then. He was a man of strength and determination with little time for words. He was a burly man, dark and powerful. A warrior husband, with a tender hand for her. She had been very young, much younger than he, when they married. I saw him bring her, trembling and uncertain, into this house.

I remember she was dressing one day, and the edge of her veil caught on his sword as she passed through the room. The snared cloth snapped her head, hurting her, and the cloth tangled as it fell. When he saw it, he was with her in an instant, caressing her head and slowly unweaving the white cloth. She stood very still and then cautiously reached around his neck. There were no words. They held each other in silence. She loved this warrior husband.

But then he was away often and for long days and nights. And when the king came with his passion and his poetry, she was confused. Her love of words and talk was ripe, and the king was full of both. The looks he gave reached her yearnings. I saw the two of them agree with their eyes as an image of poetry flew between them. They walked and talked far into the night. Yes, yes, I know! He began in lust; it is true. But he discovered more in her.

My mistress listened and offered back her own words, and when he began to do the same, well, for them there was no turning back.

And then . . . ah, you know the rest. You have heard about the pregnancy, the battle, Uriah's death. When the messenger came, my mistress would not speak to anyone. She took her husband's sword and tore all her veils. The jagged tatters fluttered on the floor for days. She would not let us gather them up. She walked through them again and again, a colored swathe of dust along the floor. She cried alone behind her door. Not even I could reach her. And when the child died, their punishment was complete.

Now she must begin the torturous journey toward forgiving. Yes, forgiving the king, forgiving herself. Only then will there be any hope of Solomon, any hope of peace.

> Another story places responsibility for David's adultery and abuse of power on other shoulders, those of Satan. These sages say that Satan appeared as a bird and when David shot an arrow at the bird, the arrow missed and hit and overturned instead Bathsheba's screen, behind which she was bathing. It was only then that David saw her beauty and wanted her. (Ginzberg IV, p. 104)

Absalom, My Enemy, My Son

David's son Absalom challenges his father for the throne. Though the king tries to protect his son's life, Absalom is killed and David grieves.

The Story

The army took the field against the Israelites, and a battle was fought in the forest of Ephron. There the Israelites were routed before the onslaught of David's men, and the loss of life was great, for twenty thousand fell. The fighting spread over the whole countryside, and the forest took toll of more people that day than the sword.

Some of David's men caught sight of Absalom; he was riding his mule and, as it passed beneath a large oak, his head was caught in its boughs; he was left in mid-air, while the mule went on from under him. One of the men who saw this told Joab, 'I saw Absalom hanging from an oak.' While the man was telling him, Joab broke in, 'You saw him? Why did you not strike him to the ground then and there? I would have given you ten pieces of silver and a belt.' The man answered, 'If you were to put into my hands a thousand pieces of silver, I would not lift a finger against the king's son; we all heard the king giving orders to you and Abishai and Ittai to take care of the young man Absalom. If I had dealt him a treacherous blow, the king would soon have known, and you would have kept well out of it.' 'That is a lie!' said Joab. 'I will make a

start and show you.' He picked up three javelins and drove them into Absalom's chest while he was held fast in the tree and still alive. Then ten young men who were Joab's armour-bearers closed in on Absalom, struck at him, and killed him. Joab sounded the trumpet, and the army came back from the pursuit of Israel, because he had called on them to halt. They took Absalom's body and flung it into a large pit in the forest, and raised over it a great cairn of stones. The Israelites all fled to their homes.

The pillar in the King's Valley had been set up by Absalom in his lifetime, for he said, 'I have no son to carry on my name.' He had named the pillar after himself, and to this day it is called Absalom's Monument.

Ahimaaz son of Zadok said, 'Let me run and take the news to the king that the LORD has avenged him and delivered him from his enemies.' But Joab replied, 'This is no day for you to be the bearer of news. Another day you may have news to carry, but not today, because the king's son is dead.' Joab told a Cushite to go and report to the king what he had seen. The Cushite bowed to Joab and set off running. Ahimaaz pleaded again with

124

Joab, 'Come what may,' he said, 'let me run after the Cushite.' 'Why should you, my son?' asked Joab. 'You will get no reward for your news.' 'Come what may,' he said, 'let me run.' 'Go, then,' said Joab. So Ahimaaz ran by the road through the plain of the Jordan and outstripped the Cushite.

David was sitting between the inner and outer gates and the watchman had gone up to the roof of the gatehouse by the wall of the town. Looking out and seeing a man running alone, the watchman called to the king and told him. 'If he is alone,' said the king, 'then he is bringing news.' The man continued to approach, and then the watchman saw another man running. He called down into the gate, 'Look, there is another man running alone.' The king said, 'He too brings news.' The watchman said, 'I see by the way he runs that the first runner is Ahimaaz son of Zadok.' The king said, 'He is a good man and shall earn the reward for good news.'

Ahimaaz called out to the king, 'All is well!' He bowed low before him and said, 'Blessed be the LORD your God who has given into your hands the men who rebelled against your majesty.' The king asked 'Is all well with the young man Absalom?' Ahimaaz answered, 'Sir, when your servant Joab sent me, I saw a great commotion, but I did not know what had happened.' The king told him to stand on one side; so he turned aside and waited there.

Then the Cushite came in and said, 'Good news for my lord the king! The LORD has avenged you this day on all those who rebelled against you.' The king said to the Cushite, 'Is all well with the young man Absalom?' The Cushite answered, 'May all the king's enemies and all rebels intent on harming you be as that young man is.' The king was deeply moved and went up to the roof-chamber over the gate and wept, crying out as he went, 'O, my son! Absalom my son, my son Absalom! Would that I had died instead of you! O Absalom, my son, my son.'

Comments on the Story

"O my son Absalom, my son, my son Absalom! Would I had died instead of you, O Absalom, my son, my son!"

Some observers say that children take on their parents' bad qualities and magnify them much more readily than they adopt their good qualities. Absalom, one of David's older sons, exemplifies this saying perfectly.

Perhaps David spoiled his children terribly and impressed upon them that the world owed them happiness, that nothing should be hard or require patience or effort. This would not be unusual for the children of a wealthy and powerful family. But one of his sons, although horribly self-absorbed, had great patience. He could wait years for the right moment to act.

Absalom's sister Tamar has told him that she was raped by her half-brother Amnon, David's oldest son, first in line to succeed their father as king. Absalom does not lash out in impulsive anger, but waits years for the moment of revenge. He invites Amnon to a party and has the unsuspecting prince murdered, thus making himself next in line to succeed to the throne.

There is clearly a sense of outrage for the violence inflicted upon his sister. He did take care of her and the half-brother who had harmed her. Absalom seems to accept society's evaluation that Amnon "ruined" Tamar when he overpowered her, and that would not be undone. Perhaps Absalom did her no favor except to see that the one who raped her did not go unpunished.

Upon his return from exile following the killing of Amnon, Absalom cannot wait for his father to die or turn over the kingdom, so he positions himself outside the gate of Jerusalem. In older tribal times this was where business and all legal transactions took place. Absalom appeals to the people's nostalgia for simpler times that no longer existed. "If only I were judge in the land! Then all who had a suit or cause might come to me, and I would give them justice" (2 Sam. 15:4).

He continues this subversion for years, until finally the time is right, and he declares himself king. He makes so many friends that David, his father, must flee for his life from the capital city with some of his wives and a few close advisers. Absalom, his father gone, publicly and ceremonially rapes David's secondary wives, a symbolic act proving that he has taken his father's (the former king's) place.

Absalom, portrayed here as someone with a cold, calculating heart, cares for no one but himself.

Then he is killed in a battle against his father's forces. While suspended by his hair in a tree in the forest, he is struck down by Joab, David's military commander. When David gets the news he cries out his grief. It is the deepest, sincerest, most gut-wrenching cry we have ever heard, and David's most authentic moment. Many people are only able to be authentically human at times of grief.

"But David," we want to say, "Absalom was evil. He tried to kill you. He had been planning it for years!"

"He was my son!" David weeps. It is the only possible response, and each parent weeps with him.

If you feel for David's grief and experience his pain, you have truly entered into this story. It presents a new side to David that he had successfully hidden previously. There is no political advantage to his open expression of grief. In fact, it hurts him politically, as his chief of staff, Joab, is bold enough to point out: "You have made it clear today that commanders and officers are nothing to you; for I perceive that if Absalom were alive and all of us were dead today, then you would be pleased" (2 Sam. 19:6).

It takes a profound tragedy such as the death of a son to strip from David his ambitious self-consciousness. Here, for the first time in a long time, David is not scheming.

Retelling the Story

In these ancient stories we hear our own voices. And the king was deeply moved and went up to the chamber over the gate, and he wept and as he went, saying: "O my son. Absalom, my son. My son Absalom, would I had died instead of you, O Absalom, my son, my son."

This David is no subject for the sentimental illustrations of a rosy mild shepherd. This David is a tormented, haggard, weeping father. This thread, this cycle of distraught grief can be found anywhere this afternoon. Somewhere in the homes of this city, listen, you will hear a cry. We know the cry too well.

A parent cries out for a lost child, and the cry covers the earth. Or a child yearns for that cry. Does my mother know me? Does my father care for me enough to cry out?

What newspaper, what street does not hold the same frantic father as this rending passage? The parent pleads for the child, "Spare him! Spare her!" The

> Absalom is described by some as being of gigantic stature. As for his hair, which was so long that it caught in a tree, some sages contend that like Samson he had taken the vows of a Nazirite (which include not cutting one's hair). So the hair that should have been the very sign of his faithfulness was the means of his death. (Ginzberg IV, pp. 104-5)

> David was so distraught at Absalom's rebellion that in his depression he was going to worship an idol, say the rabbis. When others asked him, "Should a king such as you worship an idol?" he would reply, "Should a king such as I be killed by his own son?" (Ginzberg IV, pp. 105-6)

circumstances fade, and the right and wrong of it become obscure. Who the enemy was no longer matters.

"They had not been speaking for years."

"She was into drugs."

"He loved the wrong woman."

"Well, she never did fulfill her potential."

And then the knock on the door, and life is never the same. There is the messenger and the report and the questions. How did it happen? Where was he found? Did she suffer long?

The sky is dark, and the trees shake, and time is no more. The shock comes, shattering the light, and the senses fall into empty gloom. Falling, numbness, unable to speak. He is gone and will not come again.

The questions flood in.

"What do you know about this?"

Absalom's rebellion was viewed as such a terrible breach of trust that he is one of the few Jewish ancestors who is said to have no portion in the life to come. But, it is added by some sages, each time an avenging angel attempts to punish Absalom, God stops the angel's hand. The reason is that God remembers the intense grief of David over the death of his rebellious son. (Ginzberg IV, pp. 106-7)

And the feeble reply, "All I know is. . . ."

And at last, there is no answer, only the searing grief.

The ancient storyteller gives us a cry from the rooftop that will transcend all time and place. What do our failings mean, our arguments, our rivalries? Any loss of young life tears us apart; and we run up the stairs, past the rooms where the child slept and dreamed. We run with our hearts pounding against our throats. We run with memories burning and thundering behind us.

What are memories for a father or mother who has lost a child? A comfort? A punishment? A misery? A dare? There, right over there was the place she first walked, stretching perfectly formed fingers to me. There he ran to me for comfort, and the sweet smell of his downy head shut out the world.

There was the time when she cried out for fear of death, and I hurried to her and held her. The bedroom was dark, and the bed narrow as I sat on the edge beside her.

"I am afraid to die, Mommy."

And I said, "My darling, you will not die for a long time. You will not die tonight, not tonight with my arms around you."

And there, over there are the playthings. There is the length of rope he threw up into the tree to climb and pull, his arms and legs against the rough bark of the tree. On that limb he would sit, grinning at me from the highest branch.

And later she would stand before me, angry and defiant and rebelling against everything I had thought we loved together. She yells at me and is gone. The door slams shut behind her, and now all is silence.

What of these memories? What shall we do with them? What will they do with us? They swell around us, and we run out on the roof under the night sky. The cold air slaps in around us, and the stars are steel points in the arc above us. From deep within surges a burning stream of anguish, and our bodies are racked with a cry that covers the earth.

In these ancient stories, we hear our own voices.

David's Census

David counts the people of Israel and Judah. Then he repents of having taken the census and, though many in Israel are punished, Jerusalem is spared.

The Story

Once again the Israelites felt the LORD's anger, when he incited David against them and instructed him to take a census of Israel and Judah. The king commanded Joab and the officers of the army with him to go around all the tribes of Israel, from Dan to Beersheba, and make a record of the people and report back the number to him. Joab answered, 'Even if the LORD your God should increase the people a hundredfold and your majesty should live to see it, what pleasure would that give your majesty?' But Joab and the officers, being overruled by the king, left his presence in order to take the census. . . .

After he had taken the census, David was overcome with remorse, and said to the LORD, 'I have acted very wickedly: I pray you, LORD, remove your servant's guilt, for I have been very foolish.' When he rose next morning, the command of the LORD had come to the prophet Gad, David's seer, to go and tell David: 'This is the word of the LORD: I offer you three things; choose one and I shall bring it upon you.' Gad came to David and reported this to him and said, 'Is it to be three years of famine in your land,

or three months of flight with the enemy in close pursuit, or three days of pestilence in your land? Consider carefully now what answer I am to take back to him who sent me.' David said to Gad, 'This is a desperate plight I am in; let us fall into the hands of the LORD, for his mercy is great; and let me not fall into the hands of men.'

The LORD sent a pestilence throughout Israel from the morning till the end of the appointed time; from Dan to Beersheba seventy thousand of the people died. The angel stretched out his arm towards Jerusalem to destroy it; but the LORD repented of the evil and said to the angel who was destroying the people, 'Enough! Stay your hand.' At that moment the angel of the LORD was at the threshing-floor of Araunah the Jebusite.

When David saw the angel who was striking down the people, he said to the LORD, 'It is I who have sinned, I who committed the wrong; but these poor sheep, what have they done? Let your hand fall on me and on my family.'

Gad came to David that day and said, 'Go and set up an altar to the

LORD on the threshing-floor of Arau-nah the Jebusite.' David obeyed Gad's instructions, and went up as the LORD had commanded. When Araunah looked down and saw the king and his servants coming towards him, he went out and, prostrating himself before the king, said, 'Why has your majesty come to visit his servant?' David answered, 'To buy the threshing-floor from you so that I may build an altar to the LORD, and the plague which has attacked the people may be stopped.' Araunah answered, 'I beg your majesty to take it and sacrifice what you think fit. See, here are the oxen for the whole-offering, and the threshing-sledges and the ox-yokes for fuel.' Araunah gave it all to the king for his own use and said to him, 'May the LORD your God accept you.' But the king said to Araunah, 'No, I shall buy it from you; I am not going to offer up to the LORD my God whole-offerings that have cost me nothing.' So David bought the threshing-floor and the oxen for fifty shekels of silver. He built an altar to the LORD there and offered whole-offerings and shared-offerings. Then the LORD yielded to his prayer for the land, and the plague in Israel stopped.

Comments on the Story

There is scarcely a religion that does not encourage one to obey the voice of God. In certain stories, however, God's word is not always reliable. Sometimes God will trick characters in order to hurt them, or to hurt someone else, as in the story of the census.

We are told that YHWH is angry with Israel and is seeking an excuse to punish the nation. The punishment appears to be deserved because of some unspecified sin that is part of the theological scheme in Judges—Kings. This detail of God's anger is promptly forgotten, skillfully concealed by the story-teller, who massed narrative detail but perhaps did not even know why YHWH was angry. YHWH commanded David to number his people, and David ordered that it be done.

Although surveys and the census are an established part of modern experi-ence, these activities had an entirely different reputation in the ancient world. They were related to taxation and the military draft. Joab, David's military chief of staff, recognized immediately the foolishness of David's request. By ordering a census David demonstrated a crass and cynical willingness to pre-pare to tax and conscript, two blatant violations of the ancient tribal code of Israel. Other kings counted their people, but Israel had only recently been a tribal people. They still took pride in their freedom from restrictions that a highly centralized government might place on its citizens. The thought that David might be taking away more of their rights was not only a violation of their understanding with David, but it was also looked on as a violation of YHWH's Exodus covenant with tribal Israel.

But David insisted on taking the census, confident that he had heard the voice of God, as indeed the story tells us he had. After the census was taken

(vv. 4-9), David's conscience began to bother him. The Hebrew is more graphic. "David's heart tore into him, struck him violently." He describes his act as a great sin, a foolish deed, and begs God to forgive him.

Isn't this the same God who ordered him to do it?

David is given three choices if he wants to obtain forgiveness: (1) three years of famine; (2) three months running from his enemies; or (3) three days of plague. David chooses that option that places him directly in YHWH's hands. Both famine and plague are "acts of God," but David chooses plague. David hopes a plague will end more quickly and cause less pain.

A deadly plague sweeps through Israel, and in three days 70,000 Israelites have fallen to the sickness. David, facing the horror of what he has done, begs God to desist and punish him instead.

Finally, the death angel's hand is stayed just before its sword reaches Jerusalem. The threshing floor where the plague was turned away becomes the location of Israel's temple.

But the key to understanding the story is in the first line. *God set David up.* God commanded David to do something that would inevitably begin a cycle of punishment. YHWH was angry with Israel—we never find out why, and *that* is significant. In the beginning was the anger, and all the action proceeded from that first cause, in a grim parody of the creation story. There is no apparent cause to the anger. But YHWH is not expected to visit anger upon the people unless there is just cause. So God takes advantage of a trusting servant and commands him to do something that will inevitably open Israel to punishment.

God told David to take a census so that God could punish Israel for the crime of taking a census. Suppose you heard of a father who ordered his son to make his bed before coming down to breakfast. The next morning the son makes his bed and comes down. "Did you make your bed?" the father asks. "Yes, Papa," the son replies. And the father rears back and strikes him hard in the mouth. We would quickly turn such a father over to the authorities.

This is what God is portraying as doing in this story. This may be a primitive notion of God, perhaps predating the time of Solomon's court. Later Israelite theologians refute this scheming image of God by appealing to a strict, mathematical notion of God—every human action causes an exactly measured and appropriate divine response—whether curse/punishment or blessing/reward. Such a divinity is more bloodless, less personal, but considerably less frightening and dangerous. A later retelling of this story (1 Chron. 21) portrays Satan as the instigator of the census, not YHWH. YHWH's reputation is thereby saved, and the divine fierceness is tamed.

But the appearance of an unpredictable God in a (relatively) late historical text in the Bible is an indication that this idea persisted in Israel—that God was powerful and personal but not predictable. YHWH can burst out against any people at any moment. In their ancient way, the Israelites expressed a view that the universe is not exactly balanced, that outcomes are almost always unpredictable. It was an attempt to include human pain and abandonment within the complex of religious belief.

Later theologians/writers of scripture responded that the balance would be made in some future time, rewards meted out in heaven, punishments in hell. Many ancient Israelites would rather live with the tension that God was the source not only of life but also of death and decay. We can only respect these old rabbis for looking directly into the frightening possibility that God might not be as predictable or benevolent as we would prefer.

Once again, the story is *about* the bewilderment we experience as we listen to its events. To seek to eradicate the disturbance would be to ruin the story. Rather, the storyteller's task is to connect that reaction to feelings of confusion and doubt that we experience in modern life. David's story of the census is a refined effort to explore the contours of that painful experience. Imagine how David might have felt. Frustrated? Angry? Rebellious? The text doesn't say, so we provide the motivation that seems most plausible. We do this by asking when we have felt that way.

Retelling the Story

Some say that David's sin was that he took a census without a good reason. Others say that it was because he did not pay the expected half-shekel for each person counted. Still others suggest that God made the king forget to collect the money because David had accused God of stirring up Saul's anger against him. (Ginzberg VI, p. 270; Josephus *Antiquities,* VII, 13.1)

By the stories we tell, our hallowed places were made holy. I am reminded of a story I heard years ago about a church with a blank wooden wall at the back of the pews in the congregation. Filtered light from the stained glass danced red and purple and gold along this back wall. Nothing was hung to cover the space, and it stood stark and empty as long as anyone could remember.

A few old members, when they passed the blank wall, would stop and gently bow to the vacant span. Their actions brought puzzled looks and finally questions from other church members.

"Why do you always pause and bow to that blank wall?," they wanted to know. But the old members did not know. Seems they had always nodded to that wall and had seen their parents do the same. It all appeared a senseless business, but the elder members continued, and some of the younger children began to join them.

Years passed, and when a bicentennial of the church approached, there was discussion of renovating parts of the church building. Old paint was scraped;

wood was stripped of its dark, discolored varnish; carpeting was removed. The interior of the church began to brighten and look renewed. Among the many renovation projects was the cleaning of the blank back wall. Shortly after the workers began removing the paint, they began to see colors glowing beneath the old paint. They stopped their scrubbing and told the congregation. Immediately someone called in a restoration expert from the local fine arts museum.

The woman arrived, looked at the painted panel, and then asked that the area be made available to her for a few weeks. She would have to work in a carefully controlled environment and without dust and distraction from other projects.

The congregation waited, wondering what was happening in a place they had thought of as blank and useless, a place where doting old men and women deferred to a vacant wooden wall. Children tried to peek in windows, adults planned extra meetings to examine the organ in the sanctuary, members lingered long after services to catch a glimpse of the work beneath the protective canvas sheeting over where the woman was performing her mysterious restorative rites.

Then finally one afternoon the wall was ready to be revealed. The congregation stood in the rear of the church, many in the pews, facing backward. The sun was now low in the sky, and the windows around the wall shimmered with color. Children held their parents hands, and heads inclined toward the wall.

Slowly two elders drew away the veil. A faint gasp rushed out from the gathering and then only silence. On the wooden panels was a shining painting of a resplendent Virgin and Child.

David's Death

Even a young Shunammite woman cannot stir the aged King David as he approaches the end of his days.

The Story

King David was now a very old man, and, though they wrapped clothes round him, he could not keep warm. His attendants said to him, 'Let us find a young virgin for your majesty, to attend you and take care of you; and let her lie in your arms, sir, and make you warm.' After searching throughout Israel for a beautiful maiden, they found Abishag, a Shunammite, and brought her to the king. She was a very beautiful girl. She took care of the king and waited on him, but he did not have intercourse with her. . . .

As the time of David's death drew near, he gave this charge to his son Solomon: 'I am about to go the way of all the earth. Be strong and show yourself a man. Fulfil your duty to the LORD your God; conform to his ways, observe his statutes and his commandments, his judgements and his solemn precepts, as they are written in the law of Moses, so that you may prosper in whatever you do and whichever way you turn, and that the LORD may fulfill this promise that he made about me: "If your descendants are careful to walk faithfully in my sight with all their heart and with all their soul, you shall never lack a successor on the throne of Israel."

'You know how Joab son of Zeruiah treated me and what he did to two commanders-in-chief in Israel, Abner son of Ner and Amasa son of Jether. He killed them both, breaking the peace by bloody acts of war; and with that blood he stained the belt about his waist and the sandals on his feet. Act as your wisdom prompts you, and do not let his grey hairs go down to the grave in peace. Show constant friendship to the family of Barzillai of Gilead; let them have their place at your table; they rallied to me when I was a fugitive from your brother Absalom. Do not forget Shimei son of Gera, the Benjamite from Bahurim, who cursed me bitterly the day I went to Mahanaim. True, he came down to meet me at the Jordan, and I swore by the LORD that I would not put him to death. But you do not need to let him go unpunished now; you are a wise man and will know how to deal with him; bring down his grey hairs in blood to the grave.'

So David rested with his forefathers and was buried in the city of David, having reigned over Israel for forty years, seven in Hebron and thirty-three in Jerusalem; and Solomon succeeded his father David as king and was firmly established on the throne.

Comments on the Story

In Israel and other ancient Near Eastern nations, some sages believed in "sacral kingship." For them the king embodied the fertility of the land; they believed that the assurance of a good crop yield and ever-expanding herds of livestock depended on the king's virility, his ability to perform sexually and father many children.

There were many reasons why Israelite kings had large harems. Many wives provided a means to cement political alliances with the fathers of princesses. We cannot deny that some kings saw ownership of many wives in terms of an infantile, puerile sense of fun. But the king's most important justification of the large harem was his responsibility to the principle of sacral kingship. A monarch's sexual proclivities assured the fertility of the land. If the land was fertile, crops would grow and the people would eat. The very food on the tables of the land depended at least as much on the king's sexual prowess as on his economic policy.

Thus David's sexual performance was official state business. Even in our culture, although we may not want to hear about our leaders' sexual activities, and don't approve when we do, it is still terribly important that male political candidates be perceived as "virile." Note the negative public reaction to Edmund Muskie's tears during the 1972 presidential campaign.

This narrative begins by observing that the king could no longer stay warm. The context identifies this as a euphemism for "becoming aroused." The king could no longer perform sexually, either from the degenerative effects of extreme age or because of mental incapacity.

The courtiers develop a rather ill-advised solution. They decide to put him in bed with the most beautiful woman in the kingdom, and then certainly he'll be aroused and the kingdom saved. But perhaps, in spite of all David's experience and reputation, the prospect of being in bed with a beautiful woman while all the court waits outside his bedroom door produced a rather chilling effect. Unfortunately we have uncovered the other "purpose" of a woman in this culture—to make sure that her man is aroused.

When the aged king failed to respond, Abishag, the beauty-pageant winner, must have felt a horrible failure. One could imagine her sense of inadequacy, her loss of hope and stature. David, we find, was old, tired, and a little mentally confused. It is a pathetic story, as the old king is manipulated by those around him.

His failure in this test of virility results in his two leading sons, Adonijah and Solomon, immediately positioning themselves to take over the throne. David, though failing in this vital test and thereby threatening the whole nation with drought or famine, is expected to be lucid enough to choose the new king. Only then will he be allowed to die.

Some people believe that a life can be understood or valued by the circumstances at the moment of death. Many righteous people in the Hebrew Scriptures die (as in the story of Moses) with "vigor undiminished, eyes bright and full of years" (Deut. 34:7). Of course, this belief is derived from viewing death through a particular theological lens, suggesting that this is the way righteous people should die. In truth many great people die sudden or horrible, lingering deaths, and many wicked people die as Moses did. The fact is that in each of us is a complex mixture of good and evil human qualities, so who can tell when someone's death was appropriate or deserved?

But the manner of death in any story, especially that of a king, is virtually always significant. David's death is weak and pathetic. His feeble physical condition, introduced in the first chapter of Kings, became public knowledge, and the whole place began to buzz with cross alliances, nobles promising allegiance to one or the other candidate for the throne. This was dangerous business, since to be found supporting the wrong candidate meant near-certain death.

Solomon outmaneuvered his brother Adonijah with the help of his mother, Bathsheba, and the old prophet Nathan. And in his generosity, the new King Solomon promised not to harm his brother Adonijah as long as he behaved himself.

Finally, on his deathbed, David summons his son, the king, to give him some final instructions. Would he bestow upon Solomon the fruits of his years of experience as he endeavored to be a powerful king and a faithful lover of YHWH? Would he review his mistakes for his son's instruction? Would he recount the important principles of governance?

Instead, David gives his son what amounts to a hit list, enemies to be done away with who, for various reasons, he had not killed during his lifetime. Shimei cursed him repeatedly on the day David fled to exile (see the story about Absalom). When David returned victorious, a terrified Shimei begged for his mercy, crying at David's feet, and David promised not to take revenge.

Now David tells Solomon to see to it that Shimei's "gray head does not go down to the grave in peace." David's language here employs a characteristic military euphemism for "murder."

And then there is Joab, who has been David's trusted counselor and military commander for years. When David made a bad decision, Joab did not fear to correct the king, using strong language that from another would have resulted in sure execution. When David made an ill-advised decision to take a census, Joab rebuked him sharply. "May [YHWH] your God increase the number of the people a hundredfold, while the eyes of my lord the king can still see it! But why does my lord the king want to do this?" (2 Sam. 24:3).

But at a few crucial moments, he had let David down. He had murdered Abner, his chief military rival, for command of David's armies, using as an excuse a personal vendetta. (Abner had killed Joab's brother in self-defense some time earlier.) Joab's murder of Abner destabilized the country and alienated the northern tribes, whom David so desperately tried to win over.

Finally, and most important, Joab was the one who had killed Absalom, by his own hand, when the king's son was suspended from a tree by his hair. He killed Absalom against the express orders of the king. David never forgave Joab for that. So David tells Solomon, "Let not his gray head go down to the grave in peace."

So David gave Solomon a hit list, and Solomon dutifully killed every person his father named. Then Solomon added another on his own. He killed his brother Adonijah, the one who had been his rival for the throne of Israel. This death was Solomon's idea. We can imagine that David had lost enough sons and certainly would not have favored another death in his family.

Retelling the Story

All men want one thing and one thing only. That's what I had always been told by my mother, and I had discovered that it was true on my own. So far, though, I've not given in. Oh sure, they'll tell you your hair smells like apricots while their hands search for melons elsewhere. Their lips say they admire your wit and saucy tongue while their eyes scan your robe, imagining the contours of your body beneath it. If you asked them later to repeat a single topic of your witty conversation, they couldn't do it to save their lives.

I was just a teenager when they came to me and said that I would have the "honor" of "serving" the king. I suspected then that they didn't mean serve him breakfast in bed. Besides, the rumors had already begun to fly that the king was no longer a *man,* if you know what I mean. Some of the older men began

David was destined to die on the Sabbath, according to the rabbis. When the king asked God to know the day of the week he would die, that knowledge was given to him. From that time forward, David spent each Sabbath studying the Torah in the belief that the Angel of Death could not take the life of one who was deep in study of the scriptures. One year when Shavuot (Pentecost) fell on the sabbath, the Angel of Death tricked the king. David was studying when the angel made a noise in the garden. When the king stepped out to see what it was the steps that led to the garden collapsed, killing him. People were aghast to see the king lying dead in the open, but no one could move him, since it was the sabbath. Solomon called for eagles to stand watch over the body and shade it with their wings until it could be moved. (*Ruth Rabbah* 6.2) with their superstitions, saying that this was a bad sign. If the king could not plant his seed, the fields would be as barren as old Bathsheba's womb, and the few plants that managed to break through the earth into the sun would wilt and die like the old king's shriveled desire.

I was so young and so proud of my body and my intact virginity. My parents often warned me that the clothes I chose to wear were too revealing of young flesh to be safe. But I was innocent in more ways than one. I liked the attention I received as I walked through the marketplace so much that I was never afraid. My parents were, however, so they made very sure that I never had a chance to lose my "most precious asset" (as they called it). I know now that it was their interests they were looking out for, since many an old man attempting to regain his youth would offer a handsome sum for an equally handsome young virgin.

To this day I do not know what deal was struck between the king's people and my father. One day two servants came and took me to the palace, where I was given the royal treatment. I was bathed and oiled and then given a simply cut translucent gown to wear. All the time I was being told what a great honor I had been chosen for. Then they ushered me into the king's bedroom and told the king in a louder than normal voice that I was young, beautiful (which I guess they were afraid he couldn't see for himself), and a *virgin*. They emphasized the last word with a leering tone of voice, as if that fact alone would incite the old king to rise to the occasion.

When they were sure he was conscious they left us alone. On their way out they whispered to me my instructions. I was to lie next to the king in his bed and "do whatever it takes." Then they were gone.

It is said that David lived to be seventy years old. Some rabbis tell that Adam deeded seventy of the years of his own life to his descendant. In addition, Adam gave David the gifts of beauty, poetry, and the ability to rule. (Ginzberg IV, p. 82)

There I stood, shivering in the half-darkness, surrounded by the odor of age and illness. My only thought was, "Well, let's get this thing over with." I pulled back the covers and was startled to see how thin the old king's arms and legs were. His ribs rippled under his wrinkled yellow skin, which covered what otherwise would have been a collection of bones. I was expected to raise this dry pile of sticks back to life!

I dropped my gown to the floor in as provocative a manner as I could manage. No response! I crawled into bed next to the old king and pressed my body against his, emphasizing all the right places, if you know what I mean. The king's people had instructed me in ways of holding and touching that were supposed to drive men wild, but nothing worked. My touch did not drive the king wild, but for a time I thought it had driven him mad. For some unexplainable reason he seemed to think I was his mother. I don't even want to imagine why, but he started saying, "Mommy."

Imagine that. The aged king, old enough to be my grandfather, begins rocking back and forth and saying, "Hold me, Mommy," and "Rock me, Mommy." I was scared out of my wits. I sat up and held the great King David across my lap and chest, rocking him like a baby. I had rocked my younger brothers and sisters, so when he said, "Sing to me, Mommy," I sang him the only song I knew. It was a song my grandmother sang to me when I was restless or afraid of the dark. I have no idea where she learned it, but it goes like this;

> God raises up the poor from the dirt
> and lifts up those in need from their piles of ashes.
> God seats them next to princes
> and allows them to have the seat of honor.

I had never really listened to the words until that day. As I sat there like a mother holding her newborn, who just happened to be the greatest prince in the known world, I realized the song described exactly what had happened to me. Here I was a Shunammite girl mothering the king of Israel and Judah. Then and there I knew in my heart of hearts that this had not been the work of all the king's men but of Israel's God.

To this point in my life I had only thought of what men wanted from me, and I thought I knew exactly what that was. Never before had I considered what God wanted from me. It was perfectly clear that Israel's king was no God but a man whose flesh and blood were failing fast. He would plant no more new lives in the womb of any woman, though it was still within his power to end lives. Even mine.

For now, though, the king was a child again, warm and content. I knew that my fate was not so much in his hands as it was in the same hands as his fate. I came to know that men want many things in life, not all of them from women and not all of them sexual.

Solomon's Dream

As he is about to ascend to the throne, Solomon has a dream in which God offers him a choice of gifts. Solomon chooses wisdom and then displays that wisdom when two mothers claim the same child.

The Story

Solomon himself loved the LORD, conforming to the precepts laid down by his father David; but he too slaughtered and burnt sacrifices at the shrines.

The king went to Gibeon to offer a sacrifice, for that was the chief shrine, where he used to offer a thousand whole-offerings on the altar. That night the LORD appeared to Solomon there in a dream. God said, 'What shall I give you? Tell me.' He answered, 'You have shown great and constant love to your servant David my father, because he walked before you in loyalty, righteousness, and integrity of heart; and you have maintained this great and constant love towards him and now you have given him a son to succeed him on the throne.

'Now, LORD my God, you have made your servant king in place of my father David, though I am a mere child, unskilled in leadership. Here I am in the midst of your people, the people of your choice, too many to be numbered or counted. Grant your servant, therefore, a heart with skill to listen, so that he may govern your people justly and distinguish good from evil. Otherwise who is equal to the task of governing this great people of yours?'

The Lord was well pleased that this was what Solomon had asked for, and God said, 'Because you have asked for this, and not for long life, or for wealth, or for the lives of your enemies, but have asked for discernment in administering justice, I grant your request; I give you a heart so wise and so understanding that there has been none like you before your time, nor will there be after you. What is more, I give you those things for which you did not ask, such wealth and glory as no king of your time can match. If you conform to my ways and observe my ordinances and commandments, as your father David did, I will also give you long life.' Then Solomon awoke, and realized it was a dream.

Solomon came to Jerusalem and stood before the Ark of the Covenant of the Lord, where he sacrificed whole-offerings and brought shared-offerings, and gave a banquet for all his household.

Two women who were prostitutes approached the king at that time, and as they stood before him one said, 'My lord, this woman and I share a house, and I gave birth to a child when she was there with me. On the third day after my baby was born she too gave birth to a child. We were alone; no one else was with us in the house; only the two of us were there. During the night this woman's child died because she lay on it, and she got up in the middle of the night, took my baby from my side while I, your servant, was asleep, and laid it on her bosom, putting her dead child on mine. When I got up in the morning to feed my baby, I found him dead; but when I looked at him closely, I found that it was not the child that I had borne.' The other woman broke in, 'No, the living child is mine; yours is the dead one,' while the first insisted, 'No, the dead child is yours; mine is the living one.' So they went on arguing before the king.

The king thought to himself, 'One of them says, "This is my child, the living one; yours is the dead one." The other says, "No, it is your child that is dead and mine that is alive." ' Then he said, 'Fetch me a sword.' When a sword was brought, the king gave the order: 'Cut the living child in two and give half to one woman and half to the other.' At this the woman who was the mother of the living child, moved with love for her child, said to the king, 'Oh, sir, let her have the baby! Whatever you do, do not kill it.' The other said, 'Let neither of us have it; cut it in two.' The king then spoke up: 'Give the living baby to the first woman,' he said; 'do not kill it. She is its mother.' When Israel heard the judgement which the king had given, they all stood in awe of him; for they saw that he possessed wisdom from God for administering justice.

Comments on the Story

The historian who recorded the reign of King Solomon reports that YHWH approved of his leadership, except for the fact that he continued to worship at the various cultic shrines scattered throughout Israel. In the eyes of the narrator, Solomon sinned by offering sacrifice in places other than Jerusalem. Yet in this story the most important bit of communication Solomon ever received came to him at one of these alternative altars, not Jerusalem.

Ancient people, when they wanted to receive a message from their god, would often go and sleep in a sacred site with the expectation that anything they dreamed would be in the form of a divine message. Anthropologists call this "incubation."

In this story, Solomon, a new king, somewhat insecure in his responsibilities, goes to a major "high place" at Gibeon, hoping to receive a message from YHWH. Perhaps he hoped for advice or direction to be an effective king. Imagine how startling and fearful it was when YHWH actually appeared to him in a dream and said: "Ask me for something. I'll give you whatever you want."

There are many tales throughout history where some supernatural power offers to the protagonist one or three wishes, and almost invariably the hero wastes the wishes. An ancient German folktale speaks of a peasant couple who were granted three wishes. For the first, the husband inadvertently wishes for a sausage. In response to his wife's reproach for wasting a wish on such a foolish thing, he wishes that the sausage were stuck to her nose. And finally, he must use up his third wish to relieve his wife of this gruesome appendage.

Solomon, however, is granted a single wish, and all the possibilities run through his head as the readers, too, speculate the relative advantage of each choice. Solomon could have asked for great wealth, great fame, or great power. Instead he asks for wisdom to rule. "Give your servant therefore an under-standing mind to govern your people, able to discern between good and evil; for who can govern this your great people?" (I Kings 3:9). This request so moved YHWH that Israel's God decided to grant Solomon all those other things he might have requested but didn't: wealth, fame, and power. YHWH also granted Solomon the wisdom he requested.

Almost immediately, as if to illustrate the bestowal, Solomon is presented with a thorny problem. Two women, prostitutes, approach the young king with a dispute for him to decide. In the ancient world the king was the court of final recourse. The situation was this: These women lived in the same house, and each had a baby. During the night one had accidentally smothered her child, and she subsequently switched her dead infant for the living one. Now each woman claimed the living child as her own. What sort of wisdom could YHWH give Solomon to be able to sort out this dilemma?

In a stroke of inspired genius, Solomon suggests that they cut the baby in two, giving half to one mother, half to the other. Of course, the true mother of the living child would willingly give up her offspring, rather than see it killed. This proved to be the case; the real mother offers to allow the false one to take the child in order for it to live. Thus Solomon discloses the true mother.

There remain, however, two further observations. We wonder why Solomon's first test concerns women, single parents and prostitutes. It appears that Solomon's wisdom not only separated the liar from the truthful one, but the storyteller here suggests that his insight also directed him to defend the cause of the powerless, the marginalized figures in his society. In most large, bureaucratic cultures, what high official would even listen to an argument between prostitutes? Much less the king! Who would care? A truly wise person will attend to the humanity and the rights even of those whom others consider of no great importance.

And finally, in addition to wisdom, YHWH granted Solomon fame and rich-es. Unfortunately, the fame and the riches led to Solomon's downfall. Toward the end of his career he became a ruthless dictator, abusing the rights of his people, and subject to every religious fashion. He taxed the people mercilessly to provide the needs of his opulent and profligate court, the first Israelite leader to do so. He forcibly conscripted his own people to serve on labor gangs in

Lebanon to provide building materials for his grandiose projects. And perhaps worst of all in the sight of the One from whom he had asked wisdom, Solomon worshiped other gods, rivals of YHWH for Israel's affections.

Could it be that even YHWH cannot give some individuals sufficient wisdom to handle success? Perhaps it is simply the case that humans are less able to receive and employ divine wisdom when power and success get in the way.

Retelling the Story

The young man knew that one day it might come to this. Because he was one of the sons of a great chief, the possibility was always dangling out in front of him that he would be called upon to lead his people. He had older brothers, so for many years the idea that he would become chief was only the remotest of possibilities. But his tribe was surrounded by enemies, and the buffalo were disappearing from the plains. Many went hungry or without shelter for lack of the meat and hides the buffalo provided. Many others were killed in battle. His older brothers had all fallen nobly of wounds received while defending their people. Now he was spared for this—to be the leader of his hungry, cold, war-weary people.

He went to a place in the forest where as a child he had hidden from others, a place where he felt safe. There he prayed:

Great Spirit,
  whose breath is the wind
whose tears are the dew
  I am breathless at the thought
of becoming a chief.
  My tears flow for my people
those who are hungry and cold
  those whose loved ones are gone.
I will need courage to face the years ahead.
  You, who stir courage in the hearts

Solomon had another name, Jedidiah, which means "friend of God." It was told that he came to the throne at the age of twelve. In addition to the story told in the Bible of the judgment of the case of the two women and the child, many other stories circulated about Solomon's wisdom.

Once, they say, there was a two-headed man who was the father of seven sons. One of the sons had two heads like his father. When the father died, the son with two heads claimed twice the inheritance his brothers were to receive. In order to divide the inheritance justly, Solomon had to come up with a strategy. The wise king took hot water and splashed it on one of the son's two heads. When both heads cried out in pain, Solomon discerned that this was one being with two heads, not two beings. Each son received an equal share of the inheritance. (Ginzberg IV, p. 132)

of the eagle and the mountain lion
   save courage for this chief's heart
   as well.
Great Spirit,
   who painted the sky and earth
who dressed it in the beauty of plants and creatures,
   I paint my face and wear
the feathers of a chief.
   Yet I am helpless to bring beauty
to the lives of my people.
   You, who scooped the lakes like bowls
and stood the mountains like tepees,
   give your child an eye for beauty
and a hand to create it
   as well.
Great Spirit,
   who peopled the tribes with sages and seers,
who has guided chiefs of the past in wisdom,
   my experience is small
and my knowledge is weak
   compared to your all-knowing heart.
How will I teach them to walk with compassion
   on the earth?
How will I judge them with mercy
   as well as justice?
You, who taught the fish
   the invisible paths of the stream,
teach me.
   You, who planted each growing thing
in its place,
   plant in me
a heart of wisdom.
   If you have but one gift to give,
   may it be this last, best gift.
Then he sat in silence for a long time.

Three travelers came to Solomon with this situation: They had been on a journey together when Friday afternoon came and they were forced to find a place to hide their valuables, since it was against the law to carry them on the sabbath. When they returned for their treasures, they were gone. Obviously, one of them had slipped back to their hiding place and stolen the goods. But which one?

Solomon decided to tell them a story that would reveal the guilty party. He said, "A young man and a young woman promised that they would never marry anyone else without getting the permission of the other. When they were older they lived in different towns. In her new home, the girl's father promised her hand in marriage to another young man. She went to the love of her youth to get out of their agreement, even taking money to offer him. But when he heard that she loved the new young man, he let her out of the agreement without accepting any reward from her. Her first friend simply wished her well.

While on their honeymoon, she and her husband were stopped by a robber. Before he could rob them, however, the young woman told him the story of her friend who let her out of the promise. The robber was so moved by the first young man's love for her that he took nothing from the couple, but let them go.

Solomon then turned to the travelers and asked them which character's actions they thought most noble. One said the young woman, one said the young man, and one said the robber. Solomon discerned that the one who admired the robber's actions was only interested in money and must be the thief. After further questioning, the third traveler admitted taking the valuables and showed them all where the goods were hidden. (Ginzberg IV, pp. 133-34)

Solomon Dedicates a House

Now that the temple has been completed, Solomon prays, dedicating it to YHWH.

The Story

My father David had it in mind to build a house for the name of the Lord the God of Israel, but the Lord said to him, "You purposed to build a house for my name, and your purpose was good. Nevertheless, you are not to build it; but the son who is to be born to you, he is to build the house for my name." The Lord has now fulfilled his promise: I have succeeded my father David and taken his place on the throne of Israel, as the Lord promised; and I have built the house for the name of the Lord the God of Israel. I have assigned a place in it for the Ark containing the covenant of the Lord, which he made with our forefathers when he brought them out of Egypt.'

Standing in front of the altar of the Lord in the presence of the whole assembly of Israel, Solomon spread out his hands towards heaven and said, 'Lord God of Israel, there is no God like you in heaven above or on earth beneath, keeping covenant with your servants and showing them constant love while they continue faithful to you with all their hearts. You have kept your promise to your servant David my father; by your deeds this day you have fulfilled what you said to him in words. Now, therefore, Lord God of Israel, keep this promise of yours to your servant David my father, when you said: "You will never want for a man appointed by me to sit on the throne of Israel, if only your sons look to their ways and walk before me as you have done." God of Israel, let the promise which you made to your servant David my father be confirmed.

'But can God indeed dwell on earth? Heaven itself, the highest heaven, cannot contain you; how much less this house that I have built! Yet attend, Lord my God, to the prayer and the supplication of your servant; listen to the cry and the prayer which your servant makes before you this day, that your eyes may ever be on this house night and day, this place of which you said, "My name will be there." Hear your servant when he prays towards this place. Hear the supplication of your servant and your people Israel when they pray towards this place. Hear in heaven your dwelling and, when you hear, forgive.'

Comments on the Story

Sometimes enough is enough! Solomon chose not to expand the borders of his father David's empire but decided rather to build and consolidate. Solomon never stopped developing new building projects. He built entire cities and scores of fortified settlements at the outer reaches of his father's conquered territories. He built vast storage buildings for his accumulated grain and provisions, and huge stables for his cavalry and chariot horses.

His greatest achievement was the Temple, built just outside the walls of the city of David. The Temple was a monument of the devotion to YHWH of this wealthy king. But the kind of building or monument a people build for themselves tells much about them. Compare, for instance, the stark, standing optimism of the Washington Monument, to the brutal wound in the ground known as the Vietnam Memorial. It is significant that Solomon built a Temple.

The ancient Israelite tradition pictured YHWH in a tent, because YHWH's people lived in tents. Now for years, the people had lived in houses, and it didn't seem right to have YHWH still huddled under animal skins. Even David had realized that. (See the story about David and Nathan.) But a tent could always be broken down, picked up, and moved somewhere else. It never could become completely the possession of a single tribe or a particular city or, what would be even more restrictive, a single royal family.

So even though the Ark had been an integral part of King David's royal chapel for so many years, and now it had passed on to his son Solomon, as long as it was contained in a tent there remained the possibility that it could be moved somewhere else. It didn't entirely belong to the House of David.

Solomon would now build a Temple, a shrine for the Ark in a fixed building. What few understand is that Israel, for all its wealth, still resembled what would now be known as a Third World country. The Israelites did not possess the technology to design or build such a large and complex structure, so Solomon used his wealth to import both foreign materials and skilled laborers, mostly from Tyre, a small trading nation on the coast of Palestine.

The Temple was designed to look like a Phoenician holy place (Tyre was part of Phoenicia), and Phoenician architects and engineers supervised all aspects of the project. Israelites contributed the nonskilled labor, the back work. Solomon compelled the various tribes to conscript work crews for one month out of every three. It was the first time ever that an Israelite king had actually enslaved his own people, even if just for a time.

The Temple, the pinnacle of Solomon's achievement, the ultimate expression of his building urge, was of foreign design and supervision, representing the extorted sweat of a formerly free people. And it served to fix YHWH to a particular place, belonging to a particular powerful family, Solomon's royal house. The people must have responded with some measure of ambivalence to the project.

The completed structure was another thing altogether. No one knows exactly what the building looked like, but most models represent a high rectangular building composed of dressed stone, with two free-standing pillars in the front. National pride swelled in everyone's breast, and Solomon gained a public approval rating of at least 91 percent. Everyone ate well at the dedication ceremony. The Royal Larder emptied that day, providing meat, fruit, and baked goods, as much as the people could eat, and there was still some to cart away. It was a grand party!

In the Temple itself, dramatic things happened. "The priests could not stand to serve"; YHWH was so fully present to the senses of these cultic officials.

Most of the story is taken up with Solomon's dedicatory prayer (the text is included in the common lectionary). Certainly the prayer contains all the appropriate words of thanksgiving and gratefulness for this great thing that YHWH has done. But the building of the house was designed and supervised by Baal worshiping Phoenicians, who worked with Israelite slave-labor (1 Kings 5).

Perhaps that is the very practical reason why Solomon, in his prayer, diminishes the spiritual significance of the Temple building. "But will God indeed dwell on the earth? Even heaven and the highest heaven cannot contain you, much less this house that I have built!" (1 Kings 8:27). Perhaps this was a bittersweet moment for him, in which he felt faintly guilty for the people he had used in order to build this enormous monument to YHWH. Is it possible that the Temple had become a monument not to YHWH alone but to the glory of King Solomon?

Certainly businesses and many communities of worship (often run like businesses) feel the overpowering urge to build. Often the cost of the building should be measured not in monetary value, but in the things neglected, the human considerations put aside for the fulfillment of someone's dream. Perhaps the storyteller can focus on the spiritual ambiguity of great projects, the losses incurred when any person or group endeavors to marshal significant resources for a single edifice. God certainly doesn't disparage small things. On the other hand, big things don't always impress God.

Retelling the Story

Six years ago, Cassie had become president of her alma mater, a small religious liberal arts college in an equally small town. She was the epitome of the small-town girl made good. She had grown up on the campus, where her father was professor of English literature for thirty years. She had learned jacks and hopscotch on the sidewalk outside the red brick building in which her father taught Milton, Yeats, and Eliot. She experienced her first kiss under the trees there and practiced driving on its quiet streets during times when school was not in session.

She had graduated (as everyone expected) *summa cum laude*; then it was on to graduate school. When she returned ten years after her father's retirement, she was no longer Professor Davidson's little girl. No, she was Dr. Cassandra Davidson (Ph.D. Univ. of Chicago). Prior to her homecoming she had been at various times professor, dean of students, and vice-president for student affairs at a variety of universities. When she returned to the campus that had been her childhood home, she was clearly prepared to be its president.

Cassie was not prepared, however, for what she found when she arrived. She had been told that in recent years enrollment had dropped. She knew from past experience that something would need to be done about faculty salaries, if they wanted to keep their best teachers and attract others of equal quality. Her own eyes told her that the buildings had not been kept in good repair and that no new ones had been built since her graduation. She was prepared to face these issues since they come with the territory you inherit when you assume the presidency of almost any small liberal arts college.

Two brothers lived on adjoining farms. One brother was single and the other married with children. One day the single brother began to secretly take grain from his barn and put it in his brother's barn. After all, his brother had a family to feed. At the same time, the other brother started doing exactly the same thing, bringing his grain secretly to his brother's barn. After all, his brother had no one but him and would one day be alone in the world.

One night when the moon was bright each brother was taking grain to the barn of the other when they saw each other, knew what was going on, embraced, and each laughed at the good fortune of having such a brother to care for him. It was at the very spot that the brothers met and embraced that Solomon built the Temple. (Ginzberg IV, p. 154)

What no one could have prepared her for was the true financial situation she found on arrival: a depleted endowment, a debt that seemed to grow in quantum leaps, a history of unwise investments, and worst of all the almost complete lack of support from the leaders and churches of her denomination. Any such support could be described as lukewarm, at best.

Oh, when she first arrived plenty of clergy and church leaders extended a hand and said, "We expect great things" and "If you ever need anything. . . . " A month later, though, it was next to impossible to get them to return her call. If they finally did call back, there were always the same tired voices with the same lame excuses: the building program at church, money for a director of religious education, the drive to refurbish the organ, the rise in denominational askings. To keep her anger under control and to keep from going crazy, Cassie started to play a game. She would silently guess the excuse she would hear as she waited on hold for the pastor or executive to answer. Most of the time she guessed right. This gave her some sense of satisfaction, perhaps the only thing that would come from all her calling.

Then Mr. Nakashima called her office. It seems his wife was an alumna of the school. She had been an exchange student during the years following World War II. She had described to him in glowing terms the tree-lined campus and the warm acceptance of her by the student body at a time when Japanese students were not always welcome everywhere. The Nakashimas would be coming to the States on business, and they wanted to visit the school—she for old time's sakes and he to see if all that his wife had told him could possibly be true. Cassie warned him that the buildings would not be very impressive, but the faculty was still made up of dedicated teachers and the students were still friendly, especially to those who were not always welcome outside its boundaries. In any case they were welcome, and she would be honored if they would be her guests at the president's residence.

In the car on the way back from the airport, Cassie discovered that the Nakashimas' visit was more than a walk down memory lane. Mr. Nakashima was the founder of an automotive parts company in Japan and had done very well financially. His company and its foundation were looking for investments and grant recipients. If all went as he planned, his wife's alma mater would head the list. Before they headed back to the airport to fly back to Japan, Mr. Nakashima had proposed funding a new gymnasium, a new classroom building that would contain a five hundred-seat theater, and a new chapel. In addition he would like to send one hundred Japanese students per year to the school, their education fully funded by the Nakashima Foundation. He made it clear that despite the large investment he had no desire to change the name of the school. He did, however, respectfully request that the chapel be of combined Western and Oriental design and be named for the Japanese pastor and peacemaker Toyohiko Kagawa.

> Some people complained that it was Solomon who built the Temple. They said that he was not fit for such a task, being the son of David and Bathsheba. How could God's Spirit rest upon a house built by such hands? But when the Temple was consecrated, everyone witnessed fire coming down from heaven. Then the scoffers realized they were wrong. (Ginzberg IV, p. 156)

When she returned from taking the Nakashimas to meet their flight, Cassie could hardly sleep for the excitement of it all. The very next week she announced the new plan to her denominational gathering. She was surprised and shocked by the comments of some of her "Christian" colleagues about the Japanese taking over. She started to tell them that if they had supported the college the way they should—but she didn't. She stressed that only the architect and a small portion of the materials would come from Japan. The bulk of the building materials and all the contractors and sub-contractors would be chosen locally. That would be great news for a local economy that had been doing badly for several years now.

Finally she told them that the chapel would be named The Toyohiko Kagawa Memorial Chapel. The silence and hard-edged looks spoke volumes. Her presentation ended with the question "Must Christian houses of worship all be called First Church or something equally innocuous and must all Christian people have European names for us to honor them?"

She left the words hanging in the air, returned to convince her own board of trustees, and eight months later broke ground.

> The Temple was consecrated on Yom Kippur, the Day of Atonement. All the people rejoiced, especially after a voice came from heaven, addressing all those gathered there, saying, "You shall have a portion in the world to come." (Ginzberg IV, pp. 155-56)

The Prophet from Judah

A prophet from Judah attempts to turn Jeroboam from his altar in the north, then has the tables turned on him by a less-than-trustworthy prophet from Bethel.

The Story

As Jeroboam stood by the altar to burn the sacrifice, a man of God from Judah, moved by the word of the LORD, appeared at Bethel. He inveighed against the altar in the LORD's name, crying out, 'O altar, altar! This is the word of the LORD: Listen! To the house of David a child shall be born named Josiah. On you he will sacrifice the priests of the shrines who make offerings on you, and he will burn human bones on you.' He gave a sign the same day: 'This is the sign which the LORD has ordained: This altar will be split asunder and the ashes on it will be scattered.' When King Jeroboam heard the sentence which the man of God pronounced against the altar at Bethel, he pointed to him from the altar and cried, 'Seize him! Immediately the hand which he had pointed at him became paralysed, so that he could not draw it back. The altar too was split asunder and the ashes were scattered, in fulfillment of the sign that the man of God had given at the LORD's command. The king appealed to the man of God to placate the LORD his God and pray for him that his hand might be restored. The man of

God did as he asked; the king's hand was restored and became as it had been before. He said to the man of God, 'Come home with me and have some refreshment, and let me give you a reward.' But he answered, 'If you were to give me half your house, I would not enter it with you: I will eat and drink nothing in this place, for the LORD's command to me was to eat and drink nothing, and not to go back by the way I came.' So he went back another way, not returning by the road he had taken to Bethel.

At that time there was an aged prophet living in Bethel. His sons came and told him all that the man of God had done there that day, and what he had said to the king. Their father asked, 'Which road did he take?' They pointed out the direction taken by the man of God who had come from Judah. He said to his sons, 'Saddle the donkey for me.' They saddled the donkey, and, mounted on it, he went after the man of God.

He came on him seated under a terebinth and asked, 'Are you the man of God who came from Judah?' 'I am,' he replied. 'Come home and eat with me,' said the prophet. 'I may not go back with you or enter your house,' said the other; 'I may neither eat nor drink with you in this place, for it was told me by the word of the LORD: You are to eat and drink nothing there, nor are you to go back the way you came.' The old man urged him, 'I also am a prophet, as you are; and an angel commanded me by the word of the LORD to bring you to my home to eat and drink with me.' He was lying; but the man of Judah went back with him and ate and drank in his house. While they were still seated at table the word of the LORD came to the prophet who had brought him back, and he cried out to the man of God from Judah, 'This is the word of the LORD; You have defied the word of the LORD your God and have not obeyed his command; you have gone back to eat and drink in the place where he forbade it; therefore your body will not be laid in the grave of your forefathers.'

After the man of God had eaten and drunk, the prophet who had brought him back saddled the donkey for him. As he rode on his way a lion met him and killed him, and his body was left lying in the road, with the donkey and the lion both standing beside it. Some passers-by saw the body lying in the road and the lion standing beside it, and they brought the news to the town where the old prophet lived. When the prophet who had caused him to break his journey heard it, he said, 'It is the man of God who defied the word of the LORD. The LORD has given him to the lion, and it has broken his neck and killed him in fulfilment of the word of the LORD.' He told his sons to saddle the donkey and, when they did so, he set out and found the body lying in the road with the donkey and the lion standing beside it; the lion had neither devoured the body nor broken the back of the donkey. The prophet lifted the body of the man of God, laid it on the donkey, and brought it back to his own town to mourn over it and bury it. He laid the body in his own grave and they mourned for him, saying, 'Oh, my brother!' After burying him, he said to his sons, 'When I die, bury me in the grave where the man of God lies buried, lay my bones beside his; for the sentence which he pronounced at the LORD's command against the altar in Bethel and all the temples at shrines throughout Samaria will surely come true.'

After this Jeroboam still did not abandon his evil ways, but went on appointing priests for the shrines from all classes of the people; any man who offered himself he would consecrate to be priest of a shrine. By doing this he brought guilt on his own house and doomed it to utter destruction.

Comments on the Story

In this bewildering story, it is virtually impossible to locate the voice of God. The account begins when YHWH orders a prophet from Judah, the Southern Kingdom, to move north and condemn the altar Jeroboam established to rival Solomon's Temple in Jerusalem, the capital of the Southern Kingdom. YHWH commands him not to eat, drink, or return home by the same route he came. At the very least, that would be a terrible insult to the Northerners, but also a test of this unfortunate prophet's fortitude.

The man of God from Judah challenges King Jeroboam. When the king stretches out his hand to order the prophet arrested, the hand remains paralyzed in that position. The king, now chastened, begs the Southern prophet to pray for him, which he readily does, and the king recovers. The curse upon the altar remains, however, moving toward inevitable fulfillment. The prophet, now certainly hungry and thirsty, still needs to return home, his mission accomplished. Meanwhile, word of his power spreads among the prophetic community in Bethel, the site of the condemned altar of King Jeroboam. Locally, an old prophet, also unnamed, sends word by his sons, inviting this miracle worker to his house for a meal.

The man of God from Judah, hungry, thirsty, and sorely tempted, recites his litany of obedience. "YHWH commanded me to neither eat food nor drink any water nor return the way I had come." The old prophet from Bethel has a ready rejoinder. "An angel appeared to me and told me to tell you to come to my house so you may eat." One can almost see the painful determined look melt from this Judahite's face. YHWH had seen his devotion and apparently that was sufficient. But the narrator tells us that the old prophet from Bethel was lying.

Hebrew narrative usually doesn't tell the reader how to think about a given character. Rather, the actions in the narrative demonstrate to the careful interpreter how the story should be evaluated. In these rare occasions where a bit of narrative evaluation is placed within a dramatic scene, we must pay careful attention. We have moved from the perspective of one of the characters in the story and can now see things the participants cannot. The truthfulness (or lack of it) in the characters' speech becomes a central issue in the narrative, and this parcel of information highlights this judgment. For the storyteller, such announcements should provide important hooks upon which to structure the story's development. They cannot be emphasized too much.

The man of God from Judah returns to Bethel and sits down to a long-awaited meal. But while serving, the old man, possessed by the Spirit, suddenly stands up and with fury condemns the hapless Southern prophet: "Because you have not obeyed the voice of YHWH, who commanded you not to eat or drink or go back the way you came, you will be killed by a lion." Could they possibly have finished the meal after that?

What a confusion of emotion the Judean prophet must have experienced in the final minutes before setting out to meet that lion. And the old man—what motivated him? He lied, telling the prophet to eat with him, and then condemned him for believing the lie. Why did he lie? Why did he subsequently tell the truth? Was he a false prophet who told the truth, or a true prophet who lied? Did YHWH tell him to lie, or did he do that on his own? Did YHWH inspire him to condemn the Judean prophet, or did he do *that* on his own? The psychological motives are baffling, and it gets worse. The hapless prophet

154

from Judah mounts his donkey and begins his return journey. As prophesied, a lion pounces and kills him, but leaves his body crumpled, the donkey unscathed.

When the old man hears that the prophet from Judah had died, he quickly retrieves the body and buries it in his own family tomb, with a great show of mourning. But he feels vindicated in what he had said at the dinner table, and he tells all who are willing to listen what a good prophet he is. The old man apparently feels no responsibility for the mishap.

Our sympathies cannot help remaining with the man of God from Judah, who was robbed of the satisfaction of a successful mission. It would be easy to condemn him for his weakening resolve, but each of us then would also stand condemned for not always differentiating the will of God in our day.

We notice that Israel, in this story, experiences great difficulty in locating a reliable word from YHWH. When true prophets fail to recognize false prophecy, and false prophets give true pronouncements, who can speak for God and who can know that God is speaking? Their times seem similar to our times.

When people speak, they make authoritative claims concerning their pronouncements, but the most powerful warrant would be to claim that one's words come from the very mind and intention of God. There are many ways to make such a claim, and we should take great care not to imagine that only unstable, charismatic evangelists claim to be privy to divine information. Words such as *destiny, mission,* and *absolute moral standard* all claim divine support and are subject to the winds of fashion. What a politician says, what a religious leader says, and yes, even what a storyteller says must be carefully examined according to one's previously determined standards and values. No person is above this exacting magnifying glass, no matter who she or he claims authenticated the message, or upon what divinely founded principles it stands.

Retelling the Story

(To be sung to a blues beat)
I came up from Judea.
I came a long, long way.
I came up from Judea.
I came a long, long way.
I traveled all this distance,
'Cause there's something I want to say.

There's a temple on the mountain
Somewhere to the south.
There's a temple on the mountain
Somewhere to the south.

Jeroboam continued his evil ways because the prophet from Bethel told him that the words of the prophet from Judea were false, since he was killed by a lion on his way home. (Ginzberg VI, p. 306)

From there I came to Jeroboam
To say Jere, shut your mouth.

This altar that you're building
It's just not going to do.
This altar that you're building
It's just not going to do.
YHWH told me to tell you
And YHWH's word is true.

Then just as I was leaving
Some fella called my name.
Just as I was leaving
Some fella called my name.
Said, "I'm another prophet.
You and me we're just the same."

Then he said, "Ask me no questions,
And I'll tell you no lies.
Ask me no questions,
And I'll tell you no lies.
Just join me for supper
And you'll get quite a surprise."

Let me warn you, brothers,
Watch what you say and do.
Yes, let me warn you, sisters,
Watch what you say and do.
Or you'll wind up like me
With the staring-down-the-throat-
of-a-hungry-lion blues.

Some say that the prophet from Bethel received a vision simply because he offered hospitality to the visiting prophet from Judea. Such is the power of hospitality to strangers. (Ginzberg VI, p. 306)

Elijah and the Widow at Zarephath

A widow comes to Elijah's rescue by using her meager provisions. Then the prophet returns the favor by rescuing her son from death.

The Story

Then the word of the Lord came to him: 'Go now to Zarephath, a village of Sidon, and stay there; I have commanded a widow there to feed you.' He went off to Zarephath, and when he reached the entrance to the village, he saw a widow gathering sticks. He called to her, 'Please bring me a little water in a pitcher to drink.' As she went to fetch it, he called after her, 'Bring me, please, a piece of bread as well.' But she answered, 'As the Lord your God lives, I have no food baked, only a handful of flour in a jar and a little oil in a flask. I am just gathering two or three sticks to go and cook it for my son and myself before we die.' 'Have no fear,' said Elijah; 'go and do as you have said. But first make me a small cake from what you have and bring it out to me, and after that make something for your son and yourself. For this is the word of the Lord the God of Israel: The jar of flour will not give out, nor the flask of oil fail, until the Lord sends rain on the land.' She went and did as Elijah had said, and there was food for him and for her and her family for a long time. The jar of flour did not give out, nor did the flask of oil fail, as the word of the Lord foretold through Elijah.

Afterwards the son of the woman, the owner of the house, fell ill and was in a very bad way, until at last his breathing stopped. The woman said to Elijah, 'What made you interfere, you man of God? You came here to bring my sins to light and cause my son's death!' 'Give me your son,' he said. He took the boy from her arms and carried him up to the roof-chamber where his lodging was, and laid him on his bed. He called out to the Lord, 'Lord my God, is this your care for the widow with whom I lodge, that you have been so cruel to her son?' Then he breathed deeply on the child three times and called to the Lord, 'I pray, Lord my God, let the breath of life return to the body of this child.' The Lord listened to Elijah's cry and the breath of life returned to the child's body, and he revived.

Elijah lifted him and took him down from the roof-chamber into the house, and giving him to his mother he said, 'Look, your son is alive.' She said to Elijah, 'Now I know for certain that you are a man of God and that the word of the Lord on your lips is truth.'

Comments on the Story

Jesus pointed out that when the prophet Elijah needed a place to hide out from the Israelite king who sought his life, he hid with a Phoenician woman, not an Israelite. We learn from this pronouncement that Israelites are not exclusive beneficiaries of YHWH's grace, but also that conditions had become grim in Israel, a nation that offered no protection to a prophet of YHWH.

Ahab the king had married a Phoenician princess, Jezebel, who sought to institute Baal worship as the official state religion. Elijah, whose name means "YHWH is my God," came out of the western wilderness and shut down the rain. Baal was the Phoenician storm god, bringer of the rain, so for YHWH to exercise such control over the weather was a direct insult to the power of the non-Israelite deity. In any case, the entire nation dried up.

The divinely ordained drought had spread famine and suffering beyond the borders of Israel. Elijah, when he sought a hideout from the king who blamed him, exercised an audacity that astounds, even today. "Give me all your food, and all your water," he demanded of a starving woman carrying a listless child. This stranger expected her to give him her last meal. He encouraged her sacrifice with a ringing pronouncement: "For thus says [YHWH] the god of Israel" 'The jar of meal will not be emptied and the jug of oil will not fail until the day that [YHWH] sends rain on the earth'" (1 Kings 17:14).

The woman, neither out of confidence nor out of desperation, believes the prophet. She continues to dip into her meager supplies for many days without their running out, and they all eat well for the duration of the famine. If the story ended there, we would be faced with a confident prophet caring for a sincere disciple. But the certainty in the hearts of the prophet and the woman will be challenged to the core by what follows.

When the threat of starvation has passed, the unnamed woman's son suddenly grows sick and dies. The grateful widow turns bitter. "What have you against me, O man of God? You have come to me to bring my sin to remembrance, and to cause the death of my son!" (v. 18). What a horrible mockery!— to save their lives only to snatch the boy away again. It seemed a cruel joke.

Elijah, blamed by the woman, is bewildered by the death. "O [YHWH] my God, have you brought calamity even upon the widow with whom I am staying, by killing her son?" (v. 20). In YHWH's efforts to destabilize the regime of Ahab, many innocent people have suffered, but here it has struck the prophet personally.

Elijah prays with an insistence and urgency born of his own hostility toward YHWH's decision to take the boy. He perseveres by praying on three separate occasions, lying prostrate over the lifeless body, and seemingly by a sheer act of will, calls back the boy's life again.

Prayer is such a mystery! There is such a fine line between piously accepting the will of God and responding to situations with a resolute "No!" that will not be turned aside. The Bible here portrays an individual (there are others) who will assault heaven if necessary to overcome an injustice.

Many philosophers portray God as the unmoved mover who cannot possibly change or be affected by what humans do on earth. To imagine a God capable of being influenced is (they say) to portray a deity weak and indecisive. The Bible will not allow us to portray God so coldly. Israelites were not so troubled by a God who changed his mind, and so the possibilities for human participation in the divine decision making.

Retelling the Story

"You're a demanding fellow, Elijah," the Voice said.

"You call me demanding," was the prophet's rejoinder. "Just look at all that you have asked of me."

"Well, at least I never asked for your last grains of flour and last drops of oil to make me a pancake." The Voice came back again, dripping with irony. "If I hadn't kept slipping more provisions into that widow's house, you all would have starved."

"I had faith that you would come through for the widow and semi-orphan, even if you wouldn't think of helping me. You see I know you have a soft spot for wounded types, even if they are foreigners. I knew you wouldn't let them down."

> Ahab boasted, "Didn't Moses say that YHWH wouldn't let a single drop of rain fall on the entire earth if Israel worshiped idols? Now there are idols worshiped around every corner. Why, there's hardly an idol that is not present in the land, and we have the best of everything." Elijah responded, "Your own words sealed the fate of the earth." So YHWH kept the promise made to Moses, and the heavens did not open to water the earth. (Ginzberg IV, p. 196)

Now there was a touch of incredulity in the Voice. "Well, who wouldn't be moved to mercy when you see your own prophet taking the last morsel of food out of the mouths of a widow and her child, even if they are foreigners?" The last phrase mimicked Elijah's own intonation.

"Show some mercy now, O Merciful One. I am sure it's no news to you that the child is dead. Is that what passes for mercy these days?" Elijah was irritable now, and his voice revealed it.

"I don't like your tone, Mister. Besides, you're the big-shot prophet. What do you want me to do about it?" Now the Voice was irritated, too.

"Allow me to raise the boy back to life." There was a note of pleading in the prophet's request.

"Why? So you can play the hero for the widow and get your name in the history books? Why don't you just do it yourself?" The Voice did not waver.

159

> After seeing the famine that resulted from the drought, God wanted Elijah to allow the divine promise to be set aside so that rain would fall again. To convince Elijah, God caused the prophet's favorite stream to dry up. Even then Elijah would not let God out of the promise. Then God took extreme measures. The son of the widow with whom Elijah had been staying was allowed to grow sick and die. When Elijah asked God to allow the child to live again, God agreed on the condition that the rain would fall again. Elijah agreed. Some rabbis even suggest that the son turned out to be the prophet Jonah. (Ginzberg IV, pp. 196-97)

"You know I can't do that. Anything I do comes from you. Besides, I've come to care for these two. They gave me food, took me into their family." The prophet fell silent.

The Voice spoke after a long silence, "Let me out of my promise."

"What?"

"Let me stop the drought. When this whole thing started, I thought it was a good idea to hold the rains back. You wanted to punish Ahab and Jezebel. That was not a bad idea; they needed it. But now that every human being and animal has been punished, now that even the birds, fish, and insects have been punished, it's time to stop. It's time to let the rains fall again. You made me promise to hold back the rains until your vengeance was satisfied. Let me tell you, my anger has long since been depleted. Let me out of my promise."

"Could you just let the rains fall on everyone else but Ahab and Jezebel?" The prophet was bargaining now.

"The rain will fall, when it does fall, on the just and the unjust alike. While that is not your way, it is my way." The Voice sounded adamant.

"Very well, let the rains fall. Now may I go to the boy?"

"Go to the boy," The Voice was almost musical. "Lie down upon his body with your face upon his face. Breathe upon him, and he will breathe again."

Elijah walked past the weeping widow, lay on the dead body of her son, and breathed his breath upon him. The boy stirred. From outside they all heard the slapping sound of the first huge drops of rain hitting the dry, cracked earth.

Elijah and the Priests of Baal

Elijah challenges the priests of Baal to a test to prove whose God is most powerful. YHWH wins.

The Story

So Ahab sent throughout the length and breadth of Israel and assembled the prophets on Mount Carmel.

Elijah stepped forward towards all the people there and said, 'How long will you sit on the fence? If the LORD is God, follow him; but if Baal, then follow him.' Not a word did they answer. Then Elijah said, 'I am the only prophet of the LORD still left, but there are four hundred and fifty prophets of Baal. Bring two bulls for us. Let them choose one for themselves, cut it up, and lay it on the wood without setting fire to it, and I shall prepare the other and lay it on the wood without setting fire to it. Then invoke your god by name and I shall invoke the LORD by name; the god who answers by fire, he is God.' The people all shouted their approval.

Elijah said to the prophets of Baal, 'Choose one of the bulls and offer it first, for there are more of you; invoke your god by name, but do not set fire to the wood.' They took the bull provided for them and offered it, and they invoked Baal by name from morning until noon, crying, 'Baal, answer us'; but there was no sound, no answer. They danced wildly by the altar they had set up. At midday Elijah mocked them: 'Call louder, for he is a god. It may be he is deep in thought, or engaged, or on a journey; or he may have gone to sleep and must be woken up.' They cried still louder and, as was their custom, gashed themselves with swords and spears until the blood flowed. All afternoon they raved and ranted till the hour of the regular offering, but still there was no sound, no answer, no sign of attention.

Elijah said to the people, 'Come here to me,' and they all came to him. He repaired the altar of the LORD which had been torn down. He took twelve stones, one for each tribe of the sons of Jacob, him who was named Israel by the word of the LORD. With these stones he built an altar in the name of the LORD, and dug a trench round it big enough to hold two measures of seed; he arranged the wood, cut up the bull, and laid it on the wood. Then he said, 'Fill four jars with water and pour it on the whole-offering and on the wood.' They did so; he said, 'Do it again.' They did it again; he said, 'Do it a third time.' They did it a third time, and the water ran all round the altar and even filled the trench.

At the hour of the regular offering the prophet Elijah came forward and prayed, 'LORD God of Abraham, of Isaac, and of Israel, let it be known today that you are God in Israel and that I am your servant and have done all these things at your command. Answer me, LORD, answer me and let this people know that you, LORD, are God and that it is you who have brought them back to their allegiance.' The fire of the LORD fell, consuming the whole-offering, the wood, the stones, and the earth, and licking up the water in the trench. At the sight the people all bowed with their faces to the ground and cried, 'The LORD is God, the LORD is God.' Elijah said to them, 'Seize the prophets of Baal; let not one of them escape.' They were seized, and Elijah took them down to the Kishon and slaughtered them there in the valley.

Comments on the Story

This wonderful story constitutes a triumphal victory for the forces of YHWH against his chief competitor, the Canaanite storm God, Baal.

Baal serves as a generic term for deity, the Canaanite word closest to English "Lord" or "husband" (a juxtaposition that says much about the ancient Near Eastern attitudes toward marriage). But Baal also refers to the chief of the Phoenician pantheon, the bringer of rain and fertility.

Phoenicia, with Tyre and Sidon as its chief cities, had a long paternal relationship with the kingdom of Israel. When Solomon decided to build a grand Temple for YHWH, Israel did not have the technological expertise to embark on such an ambitious project (1 Kings 5). His friend and ally, King Hiram of Tyre, lent his architects and craftspeople to design and fabricate the magnificent building. In return, Solomon provided Hiram much needed agricultural products as well as large tracts of western real estate. Our story begins years later, when to cement his nation's relationship with his more prosperous neighbor, King Omri, one of the most powerful monarchs in Israel's history, married his son Ahab to a Phoenician princess, Jezebel, the daughter of King Ith-baal. It is difficult to imagine a figure painted in as venal a fashion in biblical stories as Jezebel. She served in Israel to represent everything foreign, alien, and strange. That she was certainly a strong woman didn't help advance her reputation in vehemently patriarchal Israel.

Jezebel, it would seem from the Israelite record, made it her life's mission to promote worship of Phoenician Baal as the official religion of the kingdom of Israel, replacing YHWH. Advocates of Yahwism went underground to avoid execution by the fanatical queen. Even Elijah, YHWH's stormy prophet, went into hiding.

Then Elijah suddenly appeared with a dramatic challenge to Ahab, the prophets of Baal, and, by implication, to Queen Jezebel herself. They would all assemble on Mount Carmel, a raised area in northern Israel, jutting into the

162

Mediterranean Sea. Together they would determine which deity was a true God—that is, which deserved the loyalties of the Israelites.

In the story, Elijah proposes the ingenious test of powers, of both the prophets and the gods. They assemble two altars, one for YHWH, one for Baal. The prophet whose God can send fire down to burn up the sacrifice, bulls cut up and placed upon the altar, will be most powerful. Elijah graciously allows the 450 royal prophets of Baal to go first.

They cry out and pray to their god for most of the morning, to no avail. Elijah mocks them mercilessly. As a result, we have our most complete (although biased) picture of the intricacies and intimacies of Baal worship. They gash themselves with swords and spears until the blood flows. We imagine it would be rather hard to work up any degree of spiritual concentration, however, considering Elijah's kibitzing: "Why don't you scream louder? Perhaps he can't hear you. Maybe he's away on a trip. Maybe he's fast asleep and can't get up."

In any case, by mid-afternoon, the Baal prophets give up, sweating, bloody, and unsuccessful.

Now it is Elijah's turn. His cool confidence must have been infuriating. He begins by drenching his altar with water. The irony of this gesture is not lost on the crowd of Israelites gathered to watch the show. Elijah had ordered the rain to stop, overriding the powers of Baal, the storm god, and Israel is in the midst of a serious drought. Such profligacy with water was practically obscene!

Elijah drags out the moment with characteristic histrionics and finally calls down the fire, which boils out the water and incinerates the butchered ox.

The audience of Israelites get what they came for—a dramatic show with a clear-cut winner. They all proclaim with facile conviction: "YHWH is the true god! YHWH is the true god!" How valuable do we suppose is such a confession after such a demonstration? Where is the risk?

The story then turns grim. Elijah orders his fans to butcher the defeated Baal prophets, which they do with a frenzy and passion. They murder the prophets of Asherah (Baal's consort) as well. This tempers our initial enthusiasm for this passage.

Jezebel, of course, becomes furious when she hears what has happened. She vows to kill Elijah as he had killed her co-religionists. And Elijah is forced to run for his life into the mountains. I must, therefore, wonder how effective Elijah was, although his dramatic demonstration certainly got most of the attention and applause.

Retelling the Story

Be sure and tune in, ladies and gentlemen. See the contest of the century. You won't want to miss this one. The Great God Baal will go up against the underdog, a provincial deity who doesn't even have any vowels in his name, YHWH.

The rabbis say the priests of Baal resorted to trickery in a vain attempt to win the contest with Elijah. They tell that a man was hidden under the altar with instructions to light a fire at the first mention of Baal's name. What they didn't know was that a snake lived under the altar and on orders from YHWH bit the hidden fire-starter and killed him. When the priests shouted "Baal, Baal!" they expected the altar to burst into flame. But, as we know from the Bible story, it didn't. (Ginzberg IV, p. 198)

Here at TV-Baal you'll have a front-row seat to the most astounding event ever to be witnessed by an audience. Anyone who is anyone already has tickets to the big contest here at The Mount Carmel Arena. Not since the creation of the world has more been riding on a match. The result of tonight's contest will make a $100,000,000 purse look paltry. It'll be peanuts compared to this payoff.

The winner of tonight's match will take home a lifetime supply of prime rib entrees provided by our own Cafe Jezebel, where "all the food is fit for a god." In addition, the winner will be honored with a fiery tribute that would warm the cockles of any deity's heart and will carry away the title of Heavyweight Champion of the Universe and True God of True God.

Now entering the arena is Team Baal. They're looking sharp in their new uniforms and dancing in with that characteristic limp-step march, which is all the rage, and they're singing the Canaanite National Anthem. It's clear that this team is at the peak of their training. Sometimes we television commentators seem a bit jaded by all the money and attention we see in sports these days. But I must tell you it brings a tear to this big guy's eye to see 450 of Canaan's finest decked out fit to kill and ready to play the God Game. It's just beautiful—that's all I've got to say. Just beautiful.

Now entering the arena is Team YHWH, or however it's supposed to be pronounced. These foreign-sounding names really get me tangled up sometimes.

Since the priests of Baal were looking for a sign from their god, YHWH caused the entire universe to fall silent. The fish stopped swimming, the animals stood still and quiet, and the birds nested silently in the trees. There was not a sound in all the earth that the priests could claim was the voice of their god. (Ginzberg IV, p. 198)

Let me see, let me count to be sure. Yes, Team YHWH has only one player in today's match. That's right, it'll be one against 450. And that one player looks a little shabby. It seems to me that regulations should specify that every team should at least have uniforms in good repair, or wear a team cap or jacket or something. But I digress. I guess you don't even need a program to tell the players when there is only one. The only name I have listed here is Elijah.

164

The contest is about to begin. The coin is tossed. Team YHWH gets the toss, and their player elects to go second. Talk about confidence; this choice gives Team Baal the first strike advantage. This Elijah is pretty cocky to be a one-man team, but that's his choice.

The game has begun. Team Baal has circled the altar and have begun their limp-step dance. They are in fine form today, folks. Now they're bringing out the sharp stones and gashing their arms and legs and torsos. The blood has begun to flow, and the crowd is going wild. This is what they came to see— blood. The one member of the opposing team is harassing Team Baal. Let me remind you that this sort of harassment is traditional in the God Game. Harassing the followers of another god is a time-honored heritage in this sport.

I can just make out what he is saying above the noise of the crowd. "Where is your god? Gone on vacation? Sleeping? Gone to the bathroom?" This little guy has a lot of spirit. And it looks like he is wearing the dancers down. That's right, folks, they are definitely slowing down. Now it looks like Team Baal has called for a time out. This will give Team YHWH a chance to play.

> When Elijah began his part of the contest, everything was taking longer than he expected— building the altar, stacking the wood, and so on. In order to complete the contest the same day it began, he asked God to make the sun stand still as it had for Joshua. It did, and the contest went on as planned. (Ginzberg IV p. 199)

The single player for YHWH is talking to the officials. Oh, no! I've never heard of this one before. This Elijah wants his altar soaked with water. It's just such antics that make for the high drama of this sport. The decision is back; the judges will allow it. The altar is being soaked with water. Wait a minute, they're soaking it a second time. Hold the phone; this wood is getting a third soaking. The crowd loves this sort of tactic. This will get Team YHWH into the history books no matter the outcome of this match today.

Now that we've seen Team YHWH's bluff, let's see him show his stuff. What's this? All he's doing is rocking back and forth and mumbling. The judges will certainly give this dance routine (if you can call it that) low marks. Besides that, this crowd came to see blood, not some anemic old man doing a poor imitation of a rocking chair.

But what's this? FIRE! FIRE! Everyone out of the arena. The altar has burst into flame, and sparks and cinders are flying everywhere. The whole place is going up in flames. . . !

Elijah on Mount Horeb

Elijah encounters God in a still small voice on Mount Horeb, then goes to find a disciple who will follow in his footsteps.

The Story

When Ahab told Jezebel all that Elijah had done and how he had put all the prophets to the sword, she sent this message to Elijah, 'The gods do the same to me and more, unless by this time tomorrow I have taken your life as you took theirs.' In fear he fled for his life, and when he reached Beersheba in Judah he left his servant there, while he himself went a day's journey into the wilderness. He came to a broom bush, and sitting down under it he prayed for death: 'It is enough,' he said; 'now, LORD, take away my life, for I am no better than my fathers before me.' He lay down under the bush and, while he slept, an angel touched him and said, 'Rise and eat.' He looked, and there at his head was a cake baked on hot stones, and a pitcher of water. He ate and drank and lay down again. The angel of the LORD came again and touched him a second time, saying, 'Rise and eat; the journey is too much for you.' He rose and ate and drank and, sustained by his food, he went on for forty days and forty nights to Horeb, the mount of God. There he entered a cave where he spent the night.

The word of the LORD came to him: 'Why are you here, Elijah?' 'Because of my great zeal for the LORD the God of Hosts,' he replied. 'The people of Israel have forsaken your covenant, torn down your altars, and put your prophets to the sword. 1 alone am left, and they seek to take my life.' To this the answer came: 'Go and stand on the mount before the LORD.' The LORD was passing by: a great and strong wind came, rending mountains and shattering rocks before him, but the LORD was not in the wind; and after the wind there was an earthquake, but the LORD was not in the earthquake; and after the earthquake fire, but the LORD was not in the fire; and after the fire a faint murmuring sound. When Elijah heard it, he wrapped his face in his cloak and went out and stood at the entrance to the cave. There came a voice: 'Why are you here, Elijah?' 'Because of my great zeal for the LORD of Hosts,' he replied. 'The people of Israel have forsaken your covenant, torn down your altars, and put your prophets to the sword. I alone am left, and they seek to take my life.'

The LORD said to him, 'Go back by way of the wilderness of Damascus, enter the city, and anoint Hazael to be king of Aram; anoint also Jehu son of Nimshi to be king of Israel, and Elisha

166

son of Shaphat of Abel-meholah to be prophet in your place. Whoever escapes the sword of Hazael Jehu will slay, and whoever escapes the sword of Jehu Elisha will slay. But I shall leave seven thousand in Israel, all who have not bowed the knee to Baal, all whose lips have not kissed him.'

Elijah departed and found Elisha son of Shaphat ploughing; there were twelve pair of oxen ahead of him, and he himself was with the last of them.

As Elijah passed, he threw his cloak over him. Elisha, leaving his oxen, ran after Elijah and said, 'Let me kiss my father and mother goodbye, and then I shall follow you.' 'Go back,' he replied; 'what have I done to prevent you?' He followed him no farther but went home, took his pair of oxen, slaughtered them, and burnt the wooden yokes to cook the flesh, which he gave to the people to eat. He then followed Elijah and became his disciple.

Comments on the Story

Elijah's greatest success turned into his most profound failure. After a decisive victory over the prophets of Baal, resulting in their butchering, the great prophet of YHWH was forced to flee for his life to escape the ire of Queen Jezebel.

His southward flight (supernaturally aided) led him to the mountain where YHWH had given the law to Moses, Mount Horeb, in the Sinai. Perhaps here Elijah might find (in the place where Israel's nationhood was born) strength and healing to work against his profound discouragement. In the place where Israel found its identity, perhaps Elijah would regain his. He secured shelter in a cave and waited, hoping to find his God, who seemed so painfully absent.

What Elijah waited for will never be known, but there appeared manifestations traditionally identified with YHWH. A strong wind appeared. YHWH had spoken to the patriarch Job from the midst of a whirlwind (although a different word is used). The narrator tells us with characteristically sparse language, "God was not in the whirlwind."

Then an earthquake came, and a fire appeared. On this very mountain YHWH had spoken to Moses from a burning bush. Some time later, when YHWH gave Moses the Torah, the people saw the entire mountain encased in flame, and the earth shook under their feet. But once again, the narrator informs us "God was not in the earthquake nor the fire."

Finally, something else impinged on Elijah's consciousness. Scholars are divided as to exactly how to translate this phrase. "A still small voice" (most popular) or "a gentle quiet blowing" are two suggestions. At the very least, it was the appearance of something inconsequential, barely noticeable. The still small voice, if that is how we choose to translate it, contrasts markedly with the dramatic theophanies (manifestations of God) in a whirlwind, earthquake, or fire. And God *was* in the voice.

What remarkable insight into the continually surprising nature of YHWH! Just when we figure God out, gain sufficient influence and insight with the divine figure to create dramatic public miracles, it turns out that this elusive deity rejects all the pyrotechnics and manifests himself in a barely noticeable wisp. That's enough to disorient any prophet (and most ordinary people as well).

When Elijah finally does locate YHWH, Elijah's response is filled with self-pity and bitterness. "Everyone else has forsaken you and I alone am left." What bathos! Such whining! Is this the same great prophet who called down fire from heaven with a mere word and commanded the slaughter of hundreds of his theological opponents?

YHWH speaks quietly, parentally, to the childish man. "You are not the only one, Elijah. I have kept four thousand who have not worshiped Baal or served him." Elijah had failed to notice the many people who remained faithful in quiet, less dramatic ways, whose exploits never reached the pages of Scripture. It is encouraging to note that they too did not escape the notice of a sympathetic deity.

Then YHWH commissioned Elijah to finish his job, which required not the extermination of a few misdirected religious zealots, but the overthrow of an entire corrupt regime—the house of Omri had to go, King Ahab, Queen Jezebel, and the whole family. This job was too big for Elijah, who had burnt himself out on the one dramatic (and ineffective) demonstration on Mount Carmel. He was to appoint a successor (short-tempered Elisha) and a revolutionary leader (the military commander Jehu) to overthrow the royal house of Omri, and even to appoint a new leader of the northern neighbor to Israel, Syria, to alter the balance of power in the region.

Other than appoint a prophetic successor, Elijah accomplished none of these tasks. Others carried on his work. The days of the fierce prophet were coming to an end.

The rabbis claim that each of the events on Mount Horeb had symbolic value. The *wind* is today's world, passing as quickly as a gust of air. The *earthquake* is the day of one's death, at which people tremble. The *fire* represents sufferings that take place in Gehenna (the closest thing to hell in Hebrew thought). Then the *still small voice* was the voice of God, who alone had the last word of judgment. (Ginzberg IV, p. 200)

Retelling the Story

Darkness was her friend, an intimate companion for a long time now. It was her sanctuary, her hiding place. It was even a part of her own ebony soul, only quieter, less frightened. Night had become her sister, reflecting her own dark skin.

In the slave camps they had called her Preacher Woman. She was the most unusual of her people, a slave who could read. As a child a young mistress about her own age had taught her. This had to be accomplished in secret, of course. If their hidden lessons had been discovered, both would have been punished. It was against both law and custom to teach a slave to read.

Her textbook was the Bible, and she discovered there more than information and exercise for her newfound skill. This book opened her to a world of hopes and dreams that she had never thought possible. There she read of a God who remembered enslaved children in their suffering and led them into freedom. She heard the voice of a prophet tell of a people who had waited in darkness, only to be warmed and illuminated by a great light.

When as a young woman she was sold, her mistress gave her the Bible from which she had learned to read as a gift. She secreted it away and took it with her. At the plantation to which she was sent she would take out the Bible under the cover of night and read to any among the slave cabins who would listen the stories of the Bible. She swore all her listeners to secrecy, that they must never reveal her ability to read. They called her Preacher Woman.

She would tell them the stories of the God she read about. This was a God who listened, who felt the lashes of the slavemaster's whip along with them, who wanted more than anything to set them free. Other preachers might shout from their pulpits, but she was destined to whisper her sermons at firesides.

When they sang, it was in guarded language, words that could not be understood at the big house. "Everybody talkin' 'bout heaven ain't going," they sang. And a new song that was passing through the slave camps, "Follow the drinkin' gourd." When she slept she dreamed of a God who would sweep through the land with plagues, picking up the big houses with hands of fire and with a mighty breath blowing the cotton out of the fields like so much dandelion fluff.

Then one day the word got out, and the warning came back in panicked, whispered tones. "They've found out your secret, Preacher Woman. Men from the big house . . . coming to get you." She ran. Without even taking time to get her Bible she rushed from the camp and ran as fast as she could until darkness came. When she heard the sound of dogs and knew with a shudder that she was to be the prey of this hunt, she even ran through the darkness.

That was a week ago. Since that time she had hidden during the day and traveled at night, following the drinking gourd she had sung about so often. She had no idea whether she was still in Tennessee or had crossed the border into Kentucky. She would remain in hiding until she knew for sure that her

> Elijah is often imagined by the rabbis as serving as God's historian in paradise. He keeps records of human deeds and keeps the history of world events. He also serves as soul guide in the life to come. He takes the righteous to their appropriate places in paradise. He even brings souls from Gehenna for each Sabbath and returns them to God's presence permanently when their sins have been atoned. (Ginzberg IV, p. 201)

feet were touching the land of freedom. Each day she prayed for God to bring an earthquake or fire raining down upon those who would have her life. But all she had to comfort her were her old friends, darkness and silence.

There in the night she stared at the North Star and the handle of the Big Dipper. She listened to the silence of the starry sky. That's when it came, the still small voice. It was a barely audible whisper. It spoke one word—*freedom*.

Ahab and Naboth's Vineyard

Through deception, Jezebel seizes Naboth's vineyard and his life for her husband, Ahab. Then Elijah calls down punishment for the unscrupulous king and his house.

The Story

Some time later there occurred an incident involving Naboth of Jezreel, who had a vineyard in Jezreel adjoining the palace of King Ahab of Samaria. Ahab made a proposal to Naboth: 'Your vineyard is close to my palace; let me have it for a garden, and I shall give you a better vineyard in exchange for it or, if you prefer, I shall give you its value in silver.' But Naboth answered, 'The LORD forbid that I should surrender to you land which has always been in my family.' Ahab went home sullen and angry because Naboth had refused to let him have his ancestral holding. He took to his bed, covered his face, and refused to eat. When his wife Jezebel came in to him and asked, 'Why this sullenness, and why do you refuse to eat?' he replied, 'I proposed that Naboth of Jezreel should let me have his vineyard at its value or, if he liked, in exchange for another; but he refused to let me have it.' 'Are you or are you not king in Israel?' retorted Jezebel. 'Come, eat and take heart; I shall make you a gift of the vineyard of Naboth of Jezreel.'

She wrote letters in Ahab's name, sealed them with his seal, and sent them to the elders and notables of Naboth's city, who sat in council with him. She wrote: 'Proclaim a fast and give Naboth the seat of honour among the people. Opposite him seat two unprincipled rogues to charge him with cursing God and the king; then take him out and stone him to death.' The elders and notables of Naboth's city carried out the instructions Jezebel had sent them in her letter: they proclaimed a fast and gave Naboth the seat of honour. The two unprincipled rogues came in, sat opposite him, and charged him publicly with cursing God and the king. He was then taken outside the city and stoned, and word was sent to Jezebel that Naboth had been stoned to death.

As soon as Jezebel heard of the death of Naboth, she said to Ahab, 'Get up and take possession of the vineyard which Naboth refused to sell you, for he is no longer alive; Naboth of Jezreel is dead.'

On hearing that Naboth was dead, Ahab got up and went to the vineyard to take possession.

The word of the LORD came to Elijah the Tishbite: 'Go down at once to

171

King Ahab of Israel, who is in Samaria; you will find him in Naboth's vineyard, where he has gone to take possession. Say to him, "This is the word of the LORD: Have you murdered and seized property?" Say to him, "This is the word of the LORD: Where dogs licked the blood of Naboth, there dogs will lick your blood." ' Ahab said to Elijah, 'So you have found me, my enemy.' 'Yes,' he said, 'because you have sold yourself to do what is wrong in the eyes of the LORD. I shall bring disaster on you; I shall sweep you away and destroy every mother's son of the house of Ahab in Israel, whether under protection of the family or not. I shall deal with your house as I dealt with the house of Jeroboam son of Nebat and that of Baasha son of Ahijah, because you have provoked my anger and led Israel into sin.' The LORD went on to say of Jezebel, 'Jezebel will be eaten by dogs near the rampart of Jezreel. Of the house of Ahab, those who die in the city will be food for the dogs, and those who die in the country food for the birds.'

(Never was there a man who sold himself to do what is wrong in the LORD's eyes as Ahab did, and all at the prompting of Jezebel his wife. He committed gross abominations in going after false gods, doing everything that had been done by the Amorites, whom the LORD dispossessed in favour of Israel.)

When Ahab heard Elijah's words, he tore his clothes, put on sackcloth, and fasted; he lay down in his sackcloth and went about moaning. The word of the LORD came to Elijah the Tishbite: 'Have you seen how Ahab has humbled himself before me? Because he has thus humbled himself, I shall not bring disaster on his house in his own lifetime, but in that of his son.'

Comments on the Story

The narrator of these stories has cultivated an intense contempt and hatred for Ahab, who ruled Israel. We may find considerable merit in that storyteller's evaluation.

People who wield extraordinary power usually respond to it in one of two ways (or in some combination of the two). They either rise to the occasion and become what we tend to call statesmen (although women also need to be included in the expression), or else they lapse into a kind of immaturity that the rest of us would never be able to get away with.

Kings in the ancient Near East held virtually absolute power. Their least desires constituted the rule of law. The will of the king would inevitably be the equivalent to the will of the gods. No notion of private property or personal integrity could stand against the most insignificant whim of the king. Royal immaturity was thereby encouraged. The problem for an Israelite king was compounded, for he, in theory at least, was also a subject to a higher law: the law of YHWH.

Ahab found himself caught in the middle. Although he was an Israelite monarch, theoretically ruling by YHWH's behest, he was also part of the

Canaanite ruling class, which knew no such restrictions. His wife, the Phoenician princess Jezebel, had no patience with these kinds of narrow sectarian distinctions and felt contempt for any implied restriction upon the king's behavior.

This issue came to a head over a vineyard, belonging to a certain Naboth, which bordered on the king's property. One has to wonder how much ruling Ahab did if he had time to worry so about his precious garden. In any case, he wanted to incorporate Naboth's property with his own. It was extremely important to Ahab.

Naboth had other ideas. He represented the old-fashioned viewpoint in Israel that land was a gift of YHWH, and this land had been in his family for generations. The ancient laws even contain a provision that the land would revert to its previous owners after a set number of years, regardless of how encumbered it might have been by debt. So possession of a tract of land had theological as well as financial implications.

Naboth refused a generous offer from Ahab, and Ahab lapsed into a major sulk, lying on his bed and facing the wall. He seemed to understand the constraints on a king's action in the Israelite social structure, and he felt helpless and frustrated to do anything about it.

Jezebel, his wife, understood none of this. She was a Phoenician princess, and when her father, the King of Tyre, wanted something, he just took it. She appeared contemptuous of Ahab's perceived weakness and reminded him of his power as king over Israel. When she could not break him of his mournful attitude, she declared that she would take care of the matter herself. Such pathetic whimpering on the part of a monarch offended her sensibilities. Her manner of handling the king's business would teach Ahab a lesson, as well as instruct the horribly unsophisticated Israelites the proper way to show deference to a king.

She made short work of Naboth. She had him falsely accused of a crime, summarily executed him, and declared that his property reverted to the state. No one was the wiser, and Ahab eagerly enjoyed the fruits of his wife's manipulations. But then there was Elijah, the prophet of YHWH, spokesperson for the ancient ways of Israel.

For Elijah, this action of the royal family was the supreme violation of the nature of the Israelite social contract with YHWH. It transgressed both YHWH's sense of justice and the ancient social structure based on YHWH's law. The prophet of YHWH had no miracles for this occasion, only his scathing words of condemnation and curse. The dogs would lick Ahab's blood; the same dogs that cleaned the stones that caused Naboth's death. And once again, the dogs would feast on the corpse of Queen Jezebel.

Ahab, who had sensed the questionable nature of his enterprise from the start, was mortified by the curse, and he fell into another depressed mood. In a burst of sympathy, YHWH promised him that he would not live to see the destruction of his entire family. It would happen to Ahab's son. Thankful for small comfort, Ahab went on with his life.

Retelling the Story

Though Ahab's biblical portrait does not show him as having many virtues, certain of the rabbis take up for him. He had great respect for scholars, they say, and in his own peculiar way honored the Torah. When Benhadad had taken everything else from him, Ahab finally refused to give the Torah into his enemy's hands. In fact, when Ahab's life was examined after his death, his good deeds and evil deeds balanced each other—until, that is, the time that his treatment of Naboth was added to the evil side. That made the difference. (Ginzberg IV, p. 187)

"Ahab is not such a bad sort after all," Naboth thought to himself. "What other king would act as he has toward me? And his queen, although she is a foreigner and somewhat unorthodox in her religious practices, must be of higher character than her reputation suggests.

"I understand it is by King Ahab's own personal letter that I have been seated in the place of honor tonight. The chief elder told me so himself. And to think, just a few days ago I refused to sell the king my vineyard. He seemed so insistent at the time, but when I explained calmly and rationally that it had been in my family for generations, he let it drop. It was my impression at the time that he left in something of a snit, but I guess I was wrong. Why else would I be sitting here tonight?

"It is a truly good and righteous king who honors honesty even when that means he doesn't get everything he wants. May God bless King Ahab.

"What's that? What is such a rough looking fellow doing sitting across from the seat of honor? No! Certainly not! You misunderstood me. I would never say such a thing."

• • •

"I just hate it, hate it, hate it, hate it, HATE IT when I don't get my way. Who does Naboth think he is refusing to sell me his vineyard? Who did he think he was talking to, some local farmer? I am the king, and I thought being king meant that I got whatever I wanted. The kings in Jezebel's country certainly get everything they want. Why should I be any different from them?

"Well, I'll show them they can't treat a king this way. I just won't eat. That's what I'll do. I'll waste away to nothing till I'm the size of a dried up old leaf and just blow away. Then they'll be sorry. They won't have good old Ahab to kick around any more. They'll have to go back to kicking their mangy dogs and flea-ridden cats, because I'll be long gone.

"Who does that hick think he is? Family, schmamly. I drink wines older than his family line. Everybody has a price. It's just that his is too high, that's all. He was just trying to take advantage of my open-heartedness and good disposition. People like Naboth are a blight on society. I hate him, hate him, hate him, HATE HIM!

"Oh, I'm sorry, dear. You could hear me all the way down to your bed chamber? I'm sorry I awakened you."

• • •

"Is this man I married a king or a cockroach? It's one thing to bend and scrape to me and my wishes. After all, I'm his wife and the queen. But to let every country bumpkin get the better of him. Do I have to do everything?

"In my country things are very different. Of course, our kings don't have some jealous tribal deity breathing down their necks all the time. If they want something, they just take it. Otherwise, what's the advantage of being king?

"You see, where I come from, God is always on the king's side. I just can't adjust to a god who won't let you have whatever you want and do whatever you want. But Ahab and his people seem to have some deep-seated desire to be deprived of what they want most.

Jezebel is one of two queens who ruled in Israel. It was said that each day she weighed Ahab, and the exact weight he had gained was brought in gold and given to an idol. Apparently she never suggested that her husband go on a diet. Despite her idolatry, the rabbis have a few good things to say about Jezebel. They say she identified with the grief of others and was the chief mourner at every funeral. On the other hand, she also attended every wedding and celebrated with the happy couple and their family. (Ginzberg IV, p. 189)

That is what their God is best at, saying no. It's just a bad pattern to allow to get started, letting your God say no to you. Once you let it happen with your God, then other people think they can say no to you as well.

"I suppose I'll just have to take this thing in hand as always. Girl, tell the scribe to come to the queen's chambers. I have some letters to dictate. And be quick about it."

Micaiah Ben Imlah

When King Ahab decides to go to war, all the prophets in his kingdom assure him that YHWH is on his side and that he will win the victory—except Micaiah Ben Imlah.

The Story

The king of Israel assembled the prophets, some four hundred of them, and asked, 'Shall I attack Ramoth-gilead or not?' 'Attack,' was the answer; 'the Lord will deliver it into your majesty's hands.' Jehoshaphat asked, 'Is there no other prophet of the LORD here through whom we may seek guidance?' 'There is one more', the king of Israel answered, 'through whom we may seek guidance of the LORD, but I hate the man, because he never prophesies good for me, never anything but evil. His name is Micaiah son of Imlah.' Jehoshaphat exclaimed, 'My lord king, let no such word pass your lips!' So the king of Israel called one of his eunuchs and told him to fetch Micaiah son of Imlah with all speed.

The king of Israel and King Jehoshaphat of Judah in their royal robes were seated on their thrones at the entrance to the gate of Samaria, and all the prophets were prophesying before them. One of them, Zedekiah son of Kenaanah, made himself iron horns and declared, 'This is the word of the LORD: With horns like these you will gore the Aramaeans and make an end of them.' In the same vein all the

prophets prophesied, 'Attack Ramoth-gilead and win the day; the LORD will deliver it into your hands.'

The messenger sent to fetch Micaiah told him that the prophets had unanimously given the king a favourable answer. 'And mind you agree with them,' he added. 'As the LORD lives,' said Micaiah, 'I shall say only what the LORD tells me to say.' When he came into the king's presence, the king asked, 'Micaiah, shall I attack Ramoth-gilead, or shall I refrain?' 'Attack and win the day,' he replied; 'the LORD will deliver it into your hands.' 'How often must I adjure you', said the king, 'to tell me nothing but the truth in the name of the LORD?' Then Micaiah said,

'I saw all Israel scattered on the
    mountains,
like sheep without a shepherd;
and I heard the LORD say, "They
    have no master;
let them go home in peace." '

The king of Israel said to Jehoshaphat, 'Did I not tell you that he never prophesies good for me, never anything but evil?' Micaiah went on, 'Listen now to the word of the LORD: I saw the LORD seated on his

176

throne, with all the host of heaven in attendance on his right and on his left. The LORD said, "Who will entice Ahab to go up and attack Ramoth-gilead?" One said one thing and one said another, until a spirit came forward and, standing before the LORD, said, "I shall entice him." "How?" said the LORD. "I shall go out," he answered, "and be a lying spirit in the mouths of all his prophets." "Entice him; you will succeed," said the LORD. "Go and do it." You see, then, how the LORD has put a lying spirit in the mouths of all these prophets of yours, because he has decreed disaster for you.'

At that, Zedekiah son of Kenaanah came up to Micaiah and struck him in the face: 'And how did the spirit of the LORD pass from me to speak to you?' he demanded. Micaiah retorted, 'That you will find out on the day when you run into an inner room to hide.' The king of Israel ordered Micaiah to be arrested and committed to the custody of Amon the governor of the city and Joash the king's son. 'Throw this fellow into prison,' he said, 'and put him on a prison diet of bread and water until I come home in safety.' Micaiah declared, 'If you do return in safety, the LORD has not spoken by me.'

Comments on the Story

Micaiah prophesied at a time when prophets were plentiful. Ahab had hundreds in his royal court, every one a "yes man." When Ahab needed divine confirmation for some royal exploit, he would bring out his stable of prophets to give the "amen" to anything he planned to do. They had better, if they wanted to continue to eat at the king's table. If not, they would be prophesying on street corners for crumbs.

Micaiah had one thing the other prophets lacked: integrity. He developed a reputation for bringing bad news—that is, news that the king didn't want to hear. But Ahab kept him around anyway. Perhaps he occasionally wanted to obtain a second opinion. But mostly Micaiah was kept under wraps, not consulted. He was not popular with the other prophets.

In our story, Ahab enters an alliance with Judah (the southern Hebrew kingdom) to fight against Syria. As was their practice, two kings, brothers-in-law, consult the court prophets. With great enthusiasm, the hundreds of seers gather in a central courtyard before the thrones of the two kings and make their pronouncements.

"Go up; for [YHWH] will give it into the hand of the king" (1 Kings 22:6). Another prophet fashions a pair of iron horns and says, "With these you shall gore the Arameans [Syrians] until they are destroyed" (v. 11). Others proclaim, "Go up to Ramoth-gilead and triumph; [YHWH] will give it into the hand of the king" (v. 12). All the prophets chime in their enthusiasm. As in many mob scenes, the multitudes work themselves into a semi-hysterical state so as to engender a killing frenzy in the troops.

For some reason, the prophetic "show" did not satisfy the visiting king, whose name was Jehoshaphat. Perhaps the performance smelled false, too pat. He asks, "Don't you have any other prophets of YHWH?"

Ahab's response is immediate. He knows exactly what Jehoshaphat means. "Oh, there's Micaiah Ben Imlah, but he never prophesies good news, only bad."

"Send him in," demands Ahab's brother-in-law, the king.

Ahab takes no chances. His military guard, sent to fetch Micaiah, warns, "Now Micaiah, the other prophets all foretold victory for the king. See that you do likewise."

Micaiah replies indignantly, "I will only tell the king that YHWH instructs me." With that, he presents himself before the twin thrones. Micaiah then says plainly to the king, "Go into battle. YHWH will give you the victory," parroting the words of the other prophets.

Why does he agree with the court prophets, the yes men? Is he afraid of reprisals from the king? Has he fallen from his high calling and determination? Or does he so shape his words that the sarcasm appears obvious to all? Another more frightening possibility suggests itself, confirmed by what follows afterward: YHWH *instructs him to lie!*

In any case, Ahab sees through the charade and warns him sternly to tell only the truth when he speaks in YHWH's name.

So now is the time to talk plainly. Micaiah turns toward the kings and glared at them. He scans the countryside with his outstretched finger and intones, "I saw all Israel scattered on the mountains, like sheep that have no shepherd; and [YHWH] said, 'These have no master; let each one go home in peace' " (1 Kings 22:17). Micaiah pronounces certain death to king Ahab.

Micaiah then reports a complex vision, after which he answers the king directly. Prophets see themselves as privileged observers in the councils of heaven. Amos, a century later, claimed that YHWH did nothing without first informing his servants the prophets (Amos 3:7).

Micaiah reports on such a meeting with the heavenly council. YHWH asks his advisers, "Who will help me to deceive King Ahab?" The divine minions debate various plans, and one spirit suggests that he would enter the prophets as a lying spirit and inspire them to deceive the king. That suggestion wins the approval of YHWH, and the spirit is dispatched. So that means, in some sense, that Ahab's prophets *were* inspired by YHWH, as was Micaiah's original pronouncement to the kings.

Ahab's reaction is anti-climactic. "Do you see," he tells his fellow monarch, "he always gives bad news, just as I said." Ahab throws the rogue seer into prison. The kings ignore the prophet's advice and are both killed in a Syrian rout against the combined forces of Israel and Judah.

Theologically, this story reflects the utter despair of the Israelites of ever sorting out the complexity contained within the institution of prophecy. Ultimately, they abandoned this popular method for discerning the will of God for other seemingly more reliable methods. But the essence of the story presents the hidden God. Well-meaning (and not so well-meaning) people do their best to "tune in" to a supernatural message, but the best we have are these confusing signals, full of static. But the Israelites never gave up (nor should we) in their belief that somewhere embedded in these holy pronouncements were messages that belonged to them.

Retelling the Story

The sermon I can remember most fully out of all those I heard in my youth was on this story. To be honest, I was going through a period when I didn't want much to do with the church. I was just moving out of my teens and into my twenties, a student at Vanderbilt University. Our country was in the midst of the war with Vietnam. The region that was and is my home was emerging from a period of deep divisions over civil rights that have not yet been healed. My experience at that time led me to believe that the church had little constructive to say to such profoundly disturbing situations.

Then some friends told me about someone who was coming to preach at the university chapel. He had two strikes against him in my mind. First, he was Southern Baptist. Second, he was, like me, a Southerner. Then I happened to see him on campus during the week before he was to preach. He wore a beat-up old hat with a wide brim and had what seemed to be about three days' growth of beard. He looked more like the farmers among whom I was raised than my image of a preacher. I went to hear him.

As I sat in the chapel, listening to the opening voluntary, I looked over the order for the service until I came to the sermon title. It stopped me in my tracks. It was "Who Spread All Them Lies About Jesus?" Next to this title was the preacher's name, Will Campbell.

When the sermon began, the preacher retold the story of the king who called upon his court prophets to predict victory for him in war. And they did. Then came Micaiah, son of Imlah. He at first went along with the other prophets, and then predicted defeat and death for the king and was put in prison for it.

The rabbis say that it was not that Ahab acted against the advice and person of Micaiah that led him to destruction. No, the wheels of his fate had been set in motion much earlier, when Naboth was killed so that the king could have his vineyard. (Ginzberg IV, p. 187)

Then Campbell retold the story with a new cast of characters. The king became Richard Nixon, and the leader of the court prophets was Billy Graham.

The rabbis say that when Ahab's fate was judged, some of the heavenly hosts argued for his life to be spared, while others contended that he was a scoundrel fit for nothing but death. This is the meaning of the statement that the angels stand on God's right (life) and God's left (death). (Ginzberg VI, p. 312)

Micaiah Ben Imlah took on the dual personalities of Daniel and Philip Berrigan, who were at the time serving prison sentences for pouring blood over draft files. It was a prophetic moment for a young man who had given up on his religion. The story lived and breathed in Will Campbell's retelling.

Then the preacher began to dismantle the cultural Christianity I had rejected. After each tenet was examined he would repeat the refrain, "Who spread that lie about Jesus?"

Christians must go and kill those whom their country proclaims to be the enemy. Who spread that lie about Jesus?

The state must recognize the marriages that ministers perform in the name of Jesus. Who spread that lie?

On and on the litany went.

I left the chapel that day believing that my religion might just have something to say to a society that sought personal and national self-interest over any other values. I have never forgotten Micaiah Ben Imlah, nor have I forgotten Will Campbell. This same preacher who struggled for civil rights for African Americans also reached out to members of the Ku Klux Klan as children of God. He has gone on to record his journey of faith in books like *Brother to a Dragonfly* and *Forty Acres and a Goat*.

Since that first encounter with a true prophet of God in the preaching of Will Campbell, I have come to know and respect both far better than my limited experience would have allowed me then. And I have never shaken the suspicion that maybe, just maybe, I met two prophets that day.

Epilogue

Michael E. Williams

Those of you who have followed The Storyteller's Companion to the Bible series from its inception will notice a change in the choice and arrangement of biblical texts in subsequent volumes.

There are many methods for dividing the entire canon of the Bible into manageable portions for preaching and study. The various lectionaries from the Jewish cycle of readings for the synagogue to the *Revised Common Lectionary* lessons have been chosen to provide balanced meals week after week so the people of God would be nourished through the ongoing reading, proclaiming, and hearing "a word from God."

Jewish tradition has divided the Hebrew Scriptures into Torah, the Prophets, and the Writings. Some scholars set apart portions of the Scripture according to their literary form or genre. These include creation stories, historical narratives, poetry, prophetic utterance, apocalyptic writings, and so on. Even the most casual reader of the Bible will pick and choose those passages that seem to have the most relevance to their past experience, current life situation, or hopes for the future.

When I began work on this series, Paul Franklyn, my editor at Abingdon Press, and I set about to outline an order for these volumes that would include the major narrative portions of the Bible as well as those texts that lend themselves to narrative presentation, though they may not be a story in their original form. In volume 1, *Genesis*, we simply followed the order of stories as they appear in that book of the Bible. From the first two creation stories through the flood and the tower of Babel to the journeys of the people of God from Ur to Canaan to Egypt, the stories collected around events and persons. Along the way we met Adam and Eve, Cain and Abel, Noah and his family, Abraham and Sarah, Isaac and Rebekah, Jacob and Esau, Rachel and Leah, and finally, Joseph and his brothers. This is a family history for Jews and Christians alike, and when we leave the family they have settled in a fertile part of Egypt called Goshen.

With volume two, *Exodus—Joshua*, we pick up the story some time later when a pharaoh who does not remember Joseph and his contributions to Egypt has enslaved the Hebrew people. Here we meet Shiphrah and Puah, the midwives who refuse to do Pharaoh's murderous bidding and kill Hebrew children. We are present as God hears the cry of the people and calls Moses to lead the people out of slavery. We experience the plagues with the Egyptians and walk through the waters of the Sea of Reeds with the Israelites. We wander through the wilderness, eat manna, and receive the commandments of God with Moses. Finally we enter the promised land with Joshua.

In the present book, volume three, *Judges—Kings* we see the fledgling people of God searching for a form of leadership that will allow them to be the "blessing to all nations" for which God had set them apart. First there are the judges: the powerful woman, Deborah; the weak strongman, Samson; and the suspicious general Gideon. Disappointed with the judges and wanting to be like the other nations, the people demand a king. Gob sends Hannah's son and Eli's apprentice, Samuel, to anoint first Saul then David to the throne. We experience the mixture of triumph and tragedy in the succession of kings and those who surround them.

At this point in our outline the problem we faced was that much of the rest of the Hebrew Bible is not in narrative form. Thus subsequent volumes will be constituted by texts collected around themes or the types of literature they represent. Many of these are texts that have been neglected or completely ignored as sources for narrative preaching and teaching.

For example, one volume will collect stories of women in the Hebrew Scriptures. We will look again at some of the texts that have already been considered, but this time focusing on how they speak out of the power of the experience of women. Then there will be other texts, such as Ruth and Esther, that have too often been relegated a minor role when they deserve to stand alongside the most moving and important stories of the tradition.

Another volume will collect texts from the wisdom tradition of the Bible. It is easy to overlook the idea that many proverbs and wisdom sayings are the distilled essence of common life experiences that are most fully expressed in narratives. Many of the greatest religious insights come from life experience and have stories behind them. We hope this volume will help all of us understand that wisdom is wasted if there is no way to incorporate it in our ongoing life stories.

Future volumes will also include collections of prophetic literature and apocalyptic writings. The latter will include the Revelation to John and will serve as a bride volume to our New Testament series of The Storyteller's Companion. In this way the book that appears last in the Christian Bible can be viewed and understood alongside literature of the same type, written to serve a similar purpose: to speak of last things.

As the general editor of this series of books, I have the privilege of working with a variety of people as we prepare for each new volume. I am grateful for this opportunity and have learned from each of them. My editor, Paul

Franklyn, and copy editor, Linda Allen, have shepherded me and each volume through the paths of publishing. I appreciate more than I can say the contribution of each scholar and storyteller and the imagination and creative energy they bring to each volume. To my colleagues in the Section on Worship at the General Board of Discipleship: Verlia Burns, Hoyt Hickman, Joane Jordan, Andy Langford, and Diana Sanchez for the dreaming of this series into being along with me. As a pastor and teacher I have the luxury of two communities of imagination and support that allow these books to be grounded in the lives of people of God learning more about their biblical heritage. I am thankful for my colleagues in ministry on staff and in the congregation of Belle Meade United Methodist Church and my colleagues in learning on the faculty and in the student body of Vanderbilt Divinity School. Again, these are all my teachers.

Finally, I am grateful for you who find The Storyteller's Companion to the Bible series helpful in your lives and vocations. My hope is that these volumes will continue to ground you in the stories of faith and spark your imaginations as you see and tell of God's creative activity in creation.

Index of Readings from
The Revised Common Lectionary

1 Kings 2: 10-12; 3:3-14	Proper 15 [20]	B
1 Kings 3: 5-12	Proper 12 [17] alt.	A
1 Kings 8: (1, 6, 10-11) 22-30, 41-43	Proper 16 [21]	B
1 Kings 8:22-23, 41-43	Ninth Sunday After Epiphany	C
1 Kings 17:8-16, 17-20	Proper 5 {10]	C
1 Kings 18:20-21 (22-29) 30-39	Proper 4 [9]	C
1 Kings 19:1-4 (5-7) 8-15*a*	Proper 7 [12]	C
1 Kings 19:4-8	Proper 14 [19] alt.	B
1 Kings 21:1-10 (11-14, 15-21*a*)	Proper 6 [11]	C

Index of Midrashim